How to Find a Job as a Paralegal
A Step-by-Step Job Search Guide

Third Edition

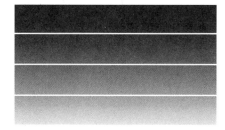

How to Find a Job as a Paralegal
A Step-by-Step Job Search Guide

Third Edition

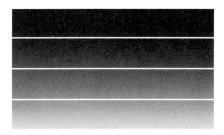

Marie Kisiel, Ph.D.
Roosevelt University

Minneapolis/St. Paul   New York   Los Angeles   San Francisco

ng
y, Inc.
graphy, Inc.

WEST'S COMMITMENT TO THE ENVIRONMENT

In 1906, West Publishing Company began recycling materials left over from the production of books. This began a tradition of efficient and responsible use of resources. Today, 100% of our legal bound volumes are printed on acid-free, recycled paper consisting of 50% new paper pulp and 50% of paper that has undergone a de-inking process. We also use vegetable-based inks to print all of our books. West recycles nearly 22,650,000 pounds of scrap paper annually—the equivalent of 187,500 trees. Since the 1960s, West has devised ways to capture and recycle waste inks, solvents, oils, and vapors created in the printing process. We also recycle plastics of all kinds, wood, glass, corrugated cardboard, and batteries, and have eliminated the use of polystyrene book packaging. We at West are proud of the longevity and the scope of our commitment to the environment.

West pocket parts and advance sheets are printed on recyclable paper and can be collected and recycled with newspapers. Staples do not have to be removed. Bound volumes can be recycled after removing the cover.

Production, Prepress, Printing and Binding by West Publishing Company.

 *TEXT IS PRINTED ON 10% POST CONSUMER RECYCLED PAPER*    Printed with **Printwise** Environmentally Advanced Water Washable Ink

British Library Cataloguing-in-Publication Data. A catalogue record for this book is available from the British Library.

Copyright © 1996   By WEST PUBLISHING COMPANY
                    610 Opperman Drive
                    P.O. Box 64526
                    St. Paul, MN 55164-0526

Library of Congress Cataloging-in-Publication Data

Kisiel, Marie.
    How to find a job as a paralegal : a step-by-step job search /
Marie Kisiel.
        p.   cm.
    Includes index.
     ISBN 0-314-06742-6 (soft : alk. paper)
     1. Legal assistants—Vocational guidance—United States.   2. Legal assistants—Employment—United States.   3. Job hunting—United States.   I. Title.
    KF320.L4K57   1996
    340′.023′73—dc20   95-39875
                                                                    CIP

Contents

Foreword

Confucius is reputed to have said, "Choose a job you love, and you will never have to work a day in your life." Such an enviable goal is not easily achieved, of course. It requires hard work, perseverance, and perhaps most importantly, self-knowledge. Few of us can claim to perceive all the motives and influences underlying our actions. The decision to undertake a career—or to change its direction—is certainly one of those crucial life choices that merits thoughtful, unhurried introspection.

It is Marie Kisiel's recognition of self-assessment as the fundamental principle of career counseling that makes her advice so timelessly valuable. I have often been privately amused how lawyer-like she can be in answering a question with another question. Her method is simply to focus on an individual's skills, accomplishments, likes, and dislikes, and then to define the resulting options so that informed career decisions can be made. This, I think, must be the basis of any successful search for satisfactory employment in these days of rapid change in an uncertain workplace.

Over the past two decades, we have heard again and again how the paralegal field is one of the "fastest-growing" occupations in America. This growth is not only in numbers, however. We are seeing what might be called a second stage in the development of the profession: an expectation of a higher level of skills, more sophisticated responsibilities, and increased emphasis on the paralegal's role as a member of the legal team. Regulation of legal assistants in some form seems probable in the near future. These circumstances make it all the more important for prospective paralegals, as well as those already working in the field, to consider carefully how their individual characteristics qualify them for a career that is likely to continue to evolve, perhaps in unexpected directions.

Marie's book helps with this task by providing extensive charts, checklists, and exercises—it is indeed a "workbook" intended to guide the reader through this self-assessment process. In particular, this new edition recognizes the increasingly varied backgrounds of paralegal students. Career changers should note that several of the sample resumes and cover letters demonstrate how experience in non-legal settings can be presented to highlight transferable skills.

Also, the expanded information on networking and job search strategies recognizes the intensified competition for good paralegal positions. Presenting a professional image has become more important, requiring among other attributes excellent listening skills, attention to matters of etiquette, and a familiarity with ethical issues. The book concludes with a new chapter on the first thirty days at a new job, offering advice and encouragement from paralegals themselves on surviving this exciting but stressful period.

Career development has been Marie's field of study throughout her academic career. Marie received her bachelor's degree from Duquesne University, her master's degree from Pennsylvania State University, and her Ph.D. from the University of Pittsburgh. She has been Professor of Humanities at Roosevelt University in Chicago for several years, teaching as well as designing specialized curricula for adult and other non-traditional students. Currently she is Academic Director of the University's Partners in Corporate Education program and Co-director of the Master of Arts in Training and Development program. In addition, she works privately as a career counselor—far too modest a title, as those of us who have benefited from her wisdom and generosity can attest. I am proud to claim her as a mentor and a cherished friend.

Jean A. Hellman
Director
Institute for Paralegal Studies
Loyola University Chicago
July, 1995

How to Use This Book

This book is designed for the paralegal who is embarking on the strenuous, challenging task of finding a job. It begins with general information on the responsibilities of a paralegal and continues with a step-by-step guide to developing skills for finding the right position in this fast-growing profession.

Depending upon your background and experience, or specific problems you may be facing in starting out as a paralegal, you may wish to focus on certain chapters. In order to gain the maximum benefit from this book, however, you should at least review each step before going on to the next one.

How to Find a Job as a Paralegal should serve as a job source guide, a professional primer, and a workbook. Use it to help understand yourself and what you have to offer the paralegal profession.

This edition offers expanded information on publications and organizations that may be valuable in the job search, and practical guidelines from experienced paralegals who've been through it. The purpose is to help you as much as possible as you begin your journey to find the job you want. Ultimately, however, the responsibility is yours.

Remember that getting a job is a skill in itself, and the person who is best prepared for that task is the one who will have the greatest success. May this book help you to achieve that goal.

Acknowledgments

I am particularly grateful to Jean Hellman, Director of the Institute for Paralegal Studies at Loyola University Chicago, for her ongoing encouragement as well as editorial insights and suggestions for this expanded edition. Linda and Phillip Exel provided valuable assistance in the earlier editions of this book, along with Cassandra Kisiel and Adrienne Hochstadt. I would also like to thank Mary Page, Manager of Legal Assistant Services at Templeton and Associates (Chicago), Illinois and Jeannine Pellettiere, Director of the Lawyer's Assistant Program at Roosevelt University (Chicago), for their comments and advice to entry-level paralegals.

I would like to acknowledge the American Bar Association, Standing Committee on Legal Assistants, for permission to reprint the definition of *legal assistant* from *The ABA Guidelines and Procedures for Obtaining ABA Approval of Legal Education Programs;* the National Association of Legal Assistants for permission to reprint the NALA Code of Ethics and Professional Responsibility; and the National Federation of Paralegal Associations for permission to reprint the NFPA Model Code of Ethics and Professional Responsibility.

I would also like to thank the following paralegal educators, who reviewed the second edition and offered comments and suggestions for improving the third edition:

Paul Dusseault
Herkimer County Community College

Tony Grindberg
Interstate Business College

Richard Kowall
University of San Francisco

Kathryn LeBlanc
Oakland University

Robert Loomis
Spokane Community College

Margaret O'Donnell
Sarasota Community Technical College

Diane Pevar
Manor Junior College

Suzanne Sheldon
Woodbury College

Richard M. Terry
Baltimore City Community College

Beverly Wilson
American Institute for Paralegal Studies, Inc.

1

Introduction

Ever since paralegals became part of the work force in the early seventies, when the American Bar Association began setting standards for paralegals, the profession has flourished, and projections indicate it will continue to do so, even in a changing work place or erratic economy.

What are the reasons for this sustained growth and the expanding opportunities for persons in this profession? A major reason is that law firms and individual attorneys have become convinced that paralegals can be very cost efficient for an organization, provided they have the education, training, and personal traits that make them assets to the organization. It is essential for the beginning paralegal to recognize these qualifications, for they are crucial factors when it comes to who gets hired and who gets ahead. As in any other profession, there is a great deal of competition for the best positions. In particular, paralegals with higher degrees and a specialized education may bring specific skills to the job and could have a competitive edge. But, in general, the prospects for all paralegals, even those with little or no experience of any kind, are very bright. It is important, however, to understand how to get off to the right start.

Let's begin by understanding the profession. Who are paralegals? What do they do? Details and information on the wide range of paralegal specialties will help you understand why paralegals are such highly prized employees.

The more you understand what paralegals do, the clearer you will be about your own options, so that you can set goals for yourself. But once you have some idea of what track you might like to follow, including a generalist track, and have attained the necessary education and training, the next stage is a crucial one. What do you do? Where do you go with what you have to offer? How do you find a job?

What is the employment scene like for paralegals? What more do you need to know about the profession and yourself to be successful in your job search? And why is it so important to be rigorous in your campaign to find a job? Where do you find opportunities? Where and how do you meet

1

people who can help you? How do you pursue job possibilities and present yourself as the best qualified candidate for the job you want?

You will find the answers in this book.

These answers will not be simple, because people from all types of backgrounds, with a wide range of experiences and a variety of credentials, are entering the field. These include students with little or no professional experience in any area; legal secretaries who are willing to obtain additional education and training; career changers, including former teachers, salespeople, artists, and insurance and realty experts; and on and on. These are the people who are attracted to the field for many reasons.

While education and training as a paralegal are becoming more and more essential, other skills are equally important. Persons with certain work habits and personality traits find the work especially rewarding and tend to be more successful than others. These are people who have strong organizational skills; can write and speak effectively; are detail-oriented; and, above all, are flexible in all aspects of their work, including work schedules.

This book will help you recognize what you need to work on in preparation for your job search. It will help you focus your skills and strengths and overcome your weaknesses. In doing so, it will help you to become the best *employed* paralegal you can be. It will serve as a step-by-step guide to help you understand the role of the paralegal and develop a job search plan that will enable you to achieve your goal of becoming a paralegal.

You will learn to identify what you have to offer: the unique talents and skills that you have developed and achievements in which you can take pride, *whatever* your background.

After a discussion of what paralegals do, including their various specialties, and what they do not do, your step-by-step guide to finding a job as a paralegal begins.

Step One involves self-assessment, which will enable you to recognize what you have achieved and what you have to offer an employer. Through a comprehensive self-inventory, you will learn how to analyze your past experiences so that you can focus on them in a resume. You will also be shown how to highlight the specific accomplishments of your academic background and how to incorporate part-time jobs, volunteer work, and internships into your professional record.

Exercises and chronological charts are included to help you recognize what you have achieved in addition to your paralegal training. Because readers' backgrounds are varied, the results will be different for each person. The important point, however, is for you to identify your own unique skills and accomplishments, whatever your background. As you do this, you will be setting the groundwork for writing a resumé that is the best reflection of you, where you have been, and what you have done. It is essential groundwork and well worth the effort you will invest.

Step Two focuses on your resumé: your professional profile. There is no one *right* way to write a resumé, and you will need to develop a resumé that works for you. The purpose of the resumé is *not* to get you the job; it is to get you the interview. Your self-assessment will prepare you for what you are to include on your resumé as a paralegal. In the resumé chapter, various formats are discussed to help you choose the best one for you. This chapter explains the categories to be included and the different options you have in presenting information about yourself on the resumé, without cluttering the pages with needless details.

"Problem areas" are also discussed in this section: how to account for long periods when you were unemployed, a wide variety of jobs you may have held, an educational or work background that may be unusual for a paralegal, limited work experience, and so forth.

How do you let the employer see your best profile without unethical padding or falsifying of information? If you have done a thorough job in planning your resumé, you can usually find more pertinent information than you may have thought of earlier in your job search.

In addition to content and format, this section also addresses the very important issue of the physical appearance of your resumé, including suggestions on paper weight and color, spacing, headings, and printing. At the end of this section, sample resumés representing a wide range of backgrounds and experiences are included.

Step Three examines the cover letter and its importance: how to individualize your letter, how to make it relevant to the resumé you have just completed, and how to tailor it to the job for which you are applying.

The cover letter will be your introduction on paper. It should make a potential employer take a closer look at your resumé and want to meet you. Several model letters in this section illustrate how you can focus on your specific skills, talents, and achievements in a short letter. To make this section even more relevant, the sample cover letters have been coordinated with sample resumés in the text.

Step Four will cover the do's and don'ts of successful interviewing. The interview will be the most stressful step of your job search. All of the work you have done so far is preparatory for this final step. How well you are prepared will frequently determine how successful you are at this stage of your job search. This section discusses how to handle this most important, and frequently most difficult, part of your entire job campaign.

You will be given suggestions to help you in your preparation, including typical interview questions and ways to rehearse answers to such questions. In addition, there is a list of questions you should ask the potential employer and guidelines on what information you should know about the position and the organization when you go to the interview.

The legalities of interviewing are also discussed in this section. It is illegal for an interviewer to ask certain questions, but, nonetheless, these questions are sometimes asked. If this happens to you during your interview, you will know how to respond. How do you negotiate a salary? How do you know when the interview is over? How can you evaluate your interview performance so you can improve your interviewing style? And what do you do next?

All of these questions are addressed in this valuable section.

Step Five will show you how to write effective follow-up letters after you have had the interview. The importance of writing these letters is stressed, and several sample letters are included.

Step Six provides an information track for you, with suggestions on how to set up your own Job Search Plan, including establishing objectives, tapping into resources, and learning to develop networking relationships. Some tips on record-keeping are also included.

The chapter on paralegal freelancing has been expanded in this edition. It discusses how to get started as a freelancer, ethical responsibilities, and tips for successful freelancing.

For those who would like to use their paralegal training and experience as a stepping stone to other careers, a chapter is included on strategies you will need to develop. You will learn how to capitalize on your skills to move into other fields and identify possible career opportunities. The purpose is to help you think about your future and make choices based on what could help you position yourself to take advantage of those options you have identified.

A final chapter has been added on practical information that will help you once you have a job: what you need to know and how to find this information. Tips from experienced paralegals are included to help you through the first days in your new position.

The **Appendices** of this book provide a list of information resources and a job notebook, as well as checklists, charts, and suggestions on how to make the best use of these materials.

Appendix A is a compilation of resources, including an outline of employers of paralegals; directories, publications, and organizations that may be helpful; information on federal jobs (including a list of Federal Job Information Centers); names and addresses of paralegal associations in the United States; additional sources of job leads; and a recommended reading list.

Appendix B includes a Job Search Notebook, along with checklists for your resumé; information on references; checklists for job sources, letters, and interviews and self-evaluation checklists and logs for your own records.

Appendix C includes the **NALA Code of Ethics and Professional Responsibility** and the **NFPA Model Code of Ethics and Professional Responsibility.**

The information in these appendices should enable you to explore the wide range of options and possibilities for your future as a paralegal. They should be a useful adjunct to the materials and strategies covered in the preceding chapters.

Keep in mind, as you go through this text, that you will have to adapt the information to your own needs and your own set of individual circumstances. From the outset we have emphasized that this book is a step-by-step guide for you. And while each chapter or section can be read separately, apart from other sections, you will benefit most by mastering each step before going on to the next one. If you are encountering problems, go back and review the points included. Try not to hurry through as you complete the exercises or reflect on the guidelines offered. Remember that finding the right job means more than just completing the paper requirements. That is just part of the job search strategy. You must approach the job search in a totally professional manner in order to become a successful paralegal. And the time and effort you invest in yourself on a personal as well as professional level will have far-reaching benefits. It will result in a successful job campaign that will lead to finding and getting the position you really want and deserve.

2

What Is a Paralegal and Why Is the Paralegal Profession Growing?

A paralegal, also known as a legal assistant, is not a lawyer but is a person who assists a lawyer in his or her professional duties. The use of paralegal services is relatively new, scarcely more than thirty years old. Like most other products and services, it developed out of a need, specifically in the 1960s when rising legal costs denied many low- and middle-income individuals access to essential legal services. That is when consumer groups, members of the organized bar, and the federal government took notice. The Legal Services Corporation was established for the purpose of providing services to those who otherwise could not afford them. Legal clinics were started, and the delivery of legal services was reevaluated with one goal in mind: How could these services be provided in a cost-efficient manner without compromising the quality of services rendered, let alone the integrity of the profession?

In addition to the adoption of more efficient management of legal services, the legal assistant was introduced. The role of the legal assistant has expanded over the years; training and education have become essential for paralegals to perform most productively in assisting lawyers.

The Definition of a Paralegal

In 1968, the The American Bar Association (ABA) established the first committee on legal assistants, endorsing the concept of paralegal practice. Since that time, the ABA *Standing Committee on Legal Assistants (ABA*

Guidelines and Procedures for Obtaining Approval of Legal Assistant Education Programs (ABA, 1987,1989,1990) has defined the role of the legal assistant as well as the parameters of the profession:

> A legal assistant is a person, qualified through education, training, or work experience, who is employed or retained by a lawyer, law office, governmental agency, or other entity in a capacity or function which involves the performance, under the ultimate direction and supervision of an attorney, of specifically delegated substantive legal work, which work, for the most part, requires a sufficient knowledge of legal concepts that, absent such an assistant, the attorney would perform the task.

This definition underscores the importance of some essential characteristics of the paralegal. First of all, it clearly explains that the paralegal does not or cannot in any way perform legal services; that is the role and responsibility of the attorney. In other words, a paralegal is a *professional* who provides legal services to the client under the *supervision* of an attorney. In order for the paralegal to assist the attorney or agency most effectively, education and training become essential qualifications, enabling the paralegal to find the best job and move ahead in the profession. And while there is currently no licensing qualification or required certification for becoming a paralegal, in a competitive job market, such credentials will assuredly enhance a person's ability to get the position.

Regulation of the Paralegal Profession

The issue of the regulation of paralegals is a topic of continuing discussion as the profession continues to grow and the responsibilities of the paralegal expand. Let's examine what such regulation would imply. First of all, there is a distinction between certification and licensure. *Certification* implies the voluntary compliance by individuals in meeting certain specifications drawn up by an agency or organization that will confer a certain designation or recognition. For example, the National Association of Legal Assistants (NALA) Certified Legal Assistant program provides a type of certification. *Licensing*, on the other hand, is a mandatory credential that an individual must obtain before practicing in certain professions. Attorneys are licensed to practice in specific states; there is no such requirement for paralegals. Many states, including California and Illinois, are, however, considering such a requirement and are studying proposed legislation. After conducting two studies and reviewing the findings, the California State Bar Association has recommended limited licensure. Other valuable studies on this topic include the following: the Cleveland Association of Paralegals Ad Hoc Committee on Limited Licensure (1989); Survey on Non-Traditional Paralegal Responsibilities (1989); and Report of the Standing Committed on the Delivery of Paralegal Services (1990). These studies are available through the National Federation of Paralegal Associations (NFPA). It is important to note that the NFPA also adopted a resolution endorsing limited licensure in 1991.

On the other hand, since 1975, the ABA has considered and reconsidered such requirements but has continued to reject such proposals with the conclusion that they are not "proper mechanisms" applicable to legal assistants.

Renewed interest in limited licensure for paralegals has been sparked with the growth of independent paralegals. In an effort to provide routine legal services directly to the public, it has been proposed that paralegals be granted permission by the state to provide services, such as real estate closings, drafting of simple wills, and selected tax services that lawyers regularly perform. One of the issues accompanying limited licensure would be strict insistence on the quality of services rendered. In other words, it would be crucial that practicing paralegals have comprehensive training, testing, and supervision.

Many paralegals already perform such duties under the supervision of attorneys. They have the education and training. Limited licensure would grant them permission to perform these tasks in direct contact with the client. Understandably, there has been resistance. Many support the concept; others believe that it will infringe upon the lawyer's territory or that the appropriate level of regulation would be difficult to define. Guidelines would have to be established for all levels of educational requirements and examinations, with built-in guarantees for monitoring quality as well as established limits of paralegal practice.

The topic is of sufficient interest that a number of states are considering it seriously. Those who favor licensure of paralegals argue that it would increase legal service costs; would not serve the public any better, since attorneys are already accountable to their clients; and would place unnecessary standardization restrictions on paralegal programs. On the other hand, licensing of paralegals would offer a new level of recognition to the profession and identify it as a legal career in itself. The debate has prompted renewed discussion from organizations and associations and, most positively, has emphasized the importance of education and training for paralegals. Much of this has resulted from the growth and involvement of paralegal associations throughout the country.

Many states have adopted guidelines for the ethical use of paralegals, including Colorado, Connecticut, Florida, Georgia, Illinois, Iowa, Kentucky, Michigan, Missouri, New Hampshire, New Mexico, New York, North Carolina, Rhode Island, South Carolina, and Texas. Some have gone so far as to include several critical areas of ethics when paralegals perform legal services directly with clients or the public. The ABA Standing Committee on Legal Assistants has established Model Guidelines for the Utilization of

Legal Assistant Services. The model is useful for states that wish to adopt guidelines to help attorneys make the most efficient as well as legal use of paralegals.

In addition, paralegal associations have prepared guidelines for their members in the code of ethics they have formulated. Both the NALA and the NFPA Association have focused on the enormous ethical responsibility of paralegals. In 1987, the NALA adopted its first Code of Ethics, with later revisions appearing in 1979, 1988, and 1995. In 1977, the NFPA adopted an Affirmation of Responsibility, with revisions made in 1981. In 1993 this was replaced by the Model Code of Ethics and Professional Responsibility. The current NALA and NFPA codes are included in Appendix C.

The impact of these guidelines has helped to establish criteria for behavior among members of the associations, and while the enforcement of the code is the domain of local chapters, the goal is to set up a high level of ethical standards for all legal assistants. Guidelines are periodically updated; as a result, they do serve a role in helping individual attorneys and state bars, as well as paralegals, to understand clearly what is considered to be ethical practice for legal assistants. Paralegal associations have also provided opportunities for professional growth and development and a networking resource. They have become a strong voice in championing the concerns of paralegals and insisting that paralegals be recognized as professionals. One area in which they have been particularly helpful is their emphasis and recommendations on educational qualifications for those entering the field.

Training Programs for Paralegals

In the early years of the profession, few training programs existed, but by 1974, the ABA adopted guidelines for an approved paralegal curriculum. Shortly after, professional paralegal associations began to spring up throughout the country. The NFPA and NALA were established. Paralegal educators soon formed their own association, the American Association for Paralegal Educators. The Legal Assistant Management Association was started by a group of paralegal supervisors and managers in 1980. A list of paralegal associations, with current addresses, are included in Appendix A of this book.

All of these organizations make a contribution to the profession; they enable professional standards to be set down and followed. As an example, in 1976, the NALA established the Certified Legal Assistant (CLA) program, a voluntary certification program consisting of two days of examinations on a variety of topics, including ethics, human relations, legal research and analysis, and four major areas of law. Certification by this program is considered a strong qualification for getting a job in many states.

What Paralegals Can and Cannot Do

Throughout the country, programs for paralegals provide intensive background and training for those preparing to assist attorneys in a wide range of activities. The scope of these activities perhaps best explains what a paralegal is. And as the profession continues to grow, so does the complexity of the tasks they perform. Many paralegals are involved in almost every aspect of a lawyer's work.

The legitimate issue, therefore, is to understand what paralegals cannot do. The cannot give legal advice, represent lawyers in court, or speak for a client. In other words, they cannot function outside the supervision of a lawyer. Later on in this chapter, a brief discussion is included on proposals that would permit paralegals to offer direct services to the client. So far this has not been approved, but it is currently under serious discussion. To avoid any illegalities, particularly when freelancing, paralegals should be aware of current legislation governing paralegal practice.

So what do paralegals do? Among a multitude of tasks and responsibilities, paralegals may do legal research, draft briefs, interview witnesses, assist at trials, file legal documents, handle real estate closings, and label documents. They may be called on, particularly in entry-level jobs, to photocopy documents, but routine clerical work is rarely the main part of their job. Legal secretaries usually perform that function along with their other office duties, particularly in a large organization. If the organization is small, the paralegal's role may differ. So, in general, the paralegal has varied responsibilities. The range of work is usually wide, depending upon the position, the setting, and the job that needs to be done. It can be exciting or it can be tedious, but is always important.

That is why paralegals are so much in demand. The work they do is essential to a lawyer. It is the time-consuming detail work that would frequently be too costly for a lawyer to perform; yet, without an efficient, reliable assistant, lawyers often cannot do their jobs. The best argument for hiring paralegals, therefore, is cost effectiveness. Legal cases are frequently so complex that it is impossible for one attorney to be a specialist in every area. Most large law firms are broken down into specialty departments such as real estate, litigation, or corporate finance. If an attorney chooses one specialty, it stands to reason that he or she will need a paralegal who is knowledgeable about that specialty.

Today, it is not unusual for a large law firm to have over one hundred lawyers on its staff, and many firms have branch offices all over the world. With expanded services and the growth of increasingly complex legal regulations, these firms continue to demand skilled paralegals. Some organizations are even moving toward a tier system for paralegals, whereby they can move up the career ladder by assuming new tasks and responsibilities.

Good performance is rewarded by advancement. For example, an Entry-Level Paralegal may become an Intermediate-Level Paralegal, and then a Senior-Level Paralegal and, depending upon the size and specialties within a firm, may advance to Case Manager (which is sometimes the same as Senior-Level Paralegal), Specialty (Corporate, Real Estate, Litigation) Support Manager, Paralegal Manager, and Paralegal Administrator. This system would vary, of course, depending upon the organization as well as the specialty. Qualifications for advancement are based on organizational standards as well as experience, skill level, education, training, and performance. A higher rank means higher pay as well as greater recognition and responsibility.

Of course, not all paralegals will choose to work in a large, often fast-paced legal environment. Many will prefer the setting of a smaller legal office or a social service agency. The person with generalist training is prepared to handle a variety of tasks, and that may be more appealing. Once a paralegal begins to explore the various specialties within the field, opportunities as well as specific interests may become more apparent.

Below is a listing of paralegal specialties, and the basic tasks they require. These will vary, of course, depending upon the organization, agency, or setting.

Areas of Specialization for Paralegals

The following listing of paralegal specialties reflects the growing trend toward specialization. Many paralegals develop specialties in several areas because of the overlapping of duties and responsibilities in those areas. Within each category, a brief description of the major paralegal duties is included. Duties and responsibilities may vary with the position. For more information and details, consult a firm, organization, or agency that handles the specialty that interests you. In all areas, of course, the paralegal works with or for an attorney. The resource list in Appendix A of this book will also provide useful information in your investigation.

Administrative Law

Government positions that handle citizen queries and complaints and draft proposed regulations and statutes for agencies. Positions are also available with law firms that represent citizens before particular agencies, including the United States Patent Office, Department of Health and Human Services, and others.

Paralegal duties include investigation, research, advocacy at agency hearings, drafting pleadings for litigation, attending hearings, and preparing reports, exhibits, or witnesses.

Admiralty Law

Law covering accidents, injuries, and deaths connected with vessels on navigable waters. Paralegal duties include investigation, research, and litigation assistance.

Antitrust Law

Paralegal work includes aspects of document control (pleadings, deposition testimony, interrogatories, and exhibits); indexing documents, drafting pleadings, investigation (statistical data and corporate structures); legal research on monopolies, marked allocation, or the Federal Trade Commission.

Banking Law and Lender Liability

Paralegal assists legal staff in such tasks as assessing bank liability for negligence claims, collection abuse, and other claims. Assists attorneys in litigating claims, monitors activities of various banking regulatory agencies, drafts and reviews loan applications and credit documents. May also analyze documents (mortgages or security agreements), arrange closings, prepare notarization of documents, monitor recordation, and conduct Uniform Commercial Code searches.

Bankruptcy Law

Paralegal interviews clients on matters of bankruptcy; reviews questionnaires on assets and liabilities. Investigates indebtedness, verifies tax liabilities, identifies creditor claims. Arranges for asset valuation, prepares inventories of assets and liabilities, opens bankruptcy petitions, and answers creditor inquiries.

Change of Name Law

Paralegal researches, gathers records, and drafts applications, files applications and pleadings in court on behalf of individuals and organizations requesting name change.

Law of Children

Paralegal works with attorney in all aspects of investigation, preliminary draftings, client counseling, legal research, and litigation assistance in cases involving adoption, child abuse, custody, paternity, and juvenile delinquency. See also *Domestic Relations Law*.

Civil Rights Law

Paralegal assists in litigation brought by citizens or law firms representing citizens in discrimination complaints, including complaints based on sex, race, religion or age.

Commercial Law Collections

Paralegal investigates claims, conducts asset checks, and verifies information. Litigation assistant in Civil Court and Small Claims Court.

Communication Law

Government paralegal assists attorneys in Federal Communications Commission work of regulating the communications industry. Assists in litigation and representation of citizens or companies in drafting applications for licenses; prepares compliance reports, exemption applications, and statistical analyses.

Construction Claims Law

Paralegal works with engineering consultant claims, including data collection, graph preparation, document preparation, and arranging for arbitration of claims.

Consumer Law

Specialty includes all aspects of consumer problems and public or private concerns that affect them: utility shutoffs, garnished wages, default judgments, lost credit cards, automobile insurance suspension, merchandise complaints, defective goods, unsatisfactory repair work, insurance claims, and so forth.Paralegals investigate, draft forms and reports, counsel clients, and assist in litigation. They also help citizens in case preparations before Small Claims Court, train other paralegals to handle consumer cases, educate community groups on consumer laws, and draft consumer-education reports.

Contract Law

All aspects of law of contract law are included in this specialty, such as antitrust law, banking law, bankruptcy law, construction law, corporate law, copyright law, domestic relations law, employee benefits law, employment law, government contract law, insurance law, international law, landlord-tenant law, oil and gas law, partnership law, real estate law, and tax law. Paralegal duties include investigation of alleged breach of contract, legal research on law of specific contracts, litigation assistance in trial of breach of contract case, and preparation of form contracts.

Copyright Law

Paralegals assist clients in copyright registration, collect data for application, file applications, prepare contracts, investigate any existing infringements, and assist in general litigation. Patent law and trademark law are related specialties.

Corporate Law

Specialty includes incorporation and corporate work, such as drafting preincorporation subscriptions, recording Articles of Incorporation, preparing documents, attending directors' meetings and drafting minutes, drafting sections of annual reports, preparing general documents, doing legal research for documents on pending legislation, preparing case profiles, monitoring law journals or newspapers, maintaining a corporate forms file,and assisting in processing patent, copyright, and trademark applications.

Criminal Law

Paralegal works for prosecutors on case reviews, police liaison, citizen complaints, consumer fraud, nonsupport and Uniform Reciprocal Enforcement of Support Act, and bad checks restitution. Serves as calendaring Aide to Calendar Court and witness liaison and helps in trial preparation. Paralegal works for defense attorneys on arranging for bail, determining of eligibility, diversion, initial client review, planning community services for clients, liaison with detained defendants, fieldwork assistance, trial preparations, plea negotiations, and appeals and collateral attacks.

Domestic Relations Law

Paralegal works with attorney in problem identification and resolution in domestic issues (divorce, law of children, and so forth.) Conducts preliminary interviews, consults with lawyers, drafts complaints, summons, judgments, and separation agreements, acts as general litigation assistant, and trains other staff.

Education Law

This field includes issues concerning school board procedures or citizen advocacy. Paralegal conducts preliminary interviews with parent or child, identifies nonlegal problems for referral to other agencies, serves as informal advocate, appears at school board meetings, and before legislative committees, attends formal hearings representing child counsel clients, and assists in litigation.

Employee Benefits Law (Qualified Plans)

Paralegals work closely with attorney, plan sponsor, administrator, and trustee in preparation and drafting of qualified employee plans. Prepares accompanying documents and monitors program, handles government compliance work, prepares and reviews annual reports of plan.

Employment Law

Paralegal identifies and investigates problems concerning individual complaints based on discrimination, demotion (or failure to promote) due to discrimination, and alleged nonpayment of salary. Prepares documents for hearing and serves as an informal advocate and negotiations mediator. Related to *Labor Law and Civil Rights Law*.

Entertainment Law

Paralegal works with different media, including television, film, radio, and print media (newspaper, book, and magazine publishers). Such work would also include contact with writers, directors, producers, and entertainers in all fields on legal issues affecting royalties, financing, and intellectual property cases.

Environmental Law

This area includes environmental protection and violation cases in all areas, including pollution (violation of pollution laws, and smoke-free environments), waste management by manufacturers, corporations, and any organization violating laws established by the Organization for Safety and Health Administration.

Family Law (Children's Rights)

Duties may include research, deposition, client interview with family members, medical personnel, legal research, and drafting documents.

Federal Government Specialties

While titles for specialties may vary within government agencies, the following indicate the primary function of the paralegal:

> Civil Rights Analyst, Employee Relations Specialist, Environmental Protection Specialist, Foreign Law Specialist, Foreign Service Diplomatic Security Officer, Freedom of Information Act Specialist, Labor Management Relations Examiner, Mediator, Security Specialist.

See Appendix A for additional information on working with the federal government.

Franchising Specialist

This speciality includes an understanding of franchise registration, trademark, and contract law.

Government Contract Law

Paralegal maintains calendar for Courts and Appeals Board, prepares claims and documents for appearances and posthearing briefs in matters concerning government contracts.

Health Law

Paralegal consults with attorney in problem identification and resolution in all aspects of legal health issues. Investigates medical records, visits sites to explore public health issues, may serve as interpreter of foreign language between medical staff and patient (explaining hospital procedures), addresses community groups on health law issues, serves as informal advocate, and assists in negotiation mediation. Appears before legislative committees or health administrative bodies to express views on healthcare issues.

Immigration Law

Paralegal identifies immigration problems, including difficulties in obtaining visa, permanent residency difficulties, nonimmigrant status, citizenship status, deportation proceedings. Provides information on visa process, residency, registration process citizenship process, and deportation process. Assists individuals in obtaining documents, refers individuals to foreign consulates or nationality organizations for assistance. Helps individuals in completing all required forms.

Insurance Law

Paralegal duties involve legal research, processing disputed benefit claims, assisting in litigation on claims brought to court, monitoring activities of insurance regulatory agencies and committees of the legislature with jurisdiction over insurance. Related to *Employee Benefits Law.*

Intellectual Property Law

This area concerns legal aspects of creative works and ideas, including manuscripts, fiction and nonfiction books, proposals, and artistic creations. Patents and copyrights are handled.

International Law

Paralegal researches, prepares, and coordinates documents and data regarding international trade, for presentation to the Commerce Department, Court of International Trade, or other governmental bodies.

Labor Law

Paralegal investigates and examines documents, assists in litigation in labor disputes before the United States Labor Relations Board, state labor relations board, and the courts. Drafts documents, arranges for depositions, and prepares statistical data, appeals, and exhibits. Relates to *Employee Benefits Law, Unemployment Compensation Law,* and *Worker's Compensation Law.*

Landlord-Tenant Law

This field includes issues relating to public and private housing. Paralegal files application for procedures, conducts preliminary interviews, drafts orders or letters requesting hearings, and serves pleadings on landlords.

Law Office Administration

Paralegal manages or supervises all aspects of personnel and office procedures. Evaluates performances, oversees accounting functions, establishes procedures for billing verification, supervises law library, establishes and maintains filing system, administers insurance programs for firm, prepares long-range budget projections, and prepares reports of individual attorneys and departments within the firm.

Legal Clinic Specialist

Paralegal performs all responsibilities and duties required in a self-help clinic, including speaking with clients, helping them to complete forms, directing questions to appropriate authorities, and, in general, providing information or assisting attorneys in any way deemed necessary.

Legislation Specialist

Paralegal monitors all events, persons, and organizations involved in passing of legislation relevant to client of firm. Drafts proposed legislation, prepares reports and studies on the subject of proposed legislation.

Litigation Specialist

Paralegal investigates, performs document research, discovery, files and serves; assists in trial preparation, and client preparation, including arranging client interviews, interviewing expert witnesses, and supervising document encodation. Assists in preparation of trial briefs, appeal documents, and other legal research.

Lobbying Specialist

Paralegal works with lobbying attorneys in research of legislative and regulatory history, monitors proposed regulations of administrative agencies and the legislature.

Medical Malpractice Law

Area requires an understanding of medical law and procedure and what constitutes malpractice. Paralegals may interview, do research, assist in preparing depositions, and speak with clients.

Mergers and Acquisitions Law

Paralegals with interest and training in corporate law may find this an appropriate specialty. Activities include research on areas such as corporate law and real estate law.

Military Law

Paralegal assists in document preparation for military proceedings, claims against the government, court reporting, and maintenance of all records.

Motor Vehicle Law

Issues concerning license suspension or revocation are the focus of this law. Paralegal assists clients in gathering records, serves as informal advocate for client with Department of Motor Vehicles and assists client in preparation of case before hearing officer in suspension or revocation of license cases.

Municipal Bonds Law

Paralegals work with attorneys specializing in banking, investment law, and regulations governing acquisition or disposition.

Oil and Gas Law

Paralegal collects and analyzes data pertaining to land ownership and activities affecting procurement of rights to explore or drill for and produce oil or gas. Helps to acquire leases and monitors execution of leases and other agreements; helps to negotiate agreements, processes and monitors termination of leases and agreements, and examines land titles. See also *Real Estate Law.*

Parajudge

In states where judges in certain lower courts are not required to be attorneys (local magistrate courts, Justice of the Peace courts), paralegals may have limited roles in conducting designated pretrial proceedings and making recommendations to regular court.

Partnership Law

Paralegal drafts preorganization agreement and records minutes of meetings and agreements for dissolution of partnership. Drafts and publishes notice of termination of partnership, drafts noncompetitive agreements for selling partners, and drafts assignment of partnership interests.

Patent Law

Paralegal helps inventor apply for a patent with the United States Patent and Trademark Office, conducts patent search, monitors responses from government offices, helps market invention by identifying licenses, studies market, prepares contracts, and investigates patent infringements.

Personal Injury Law

Paralegal handles all aspects of personal injury claims, including interviewing witnesses, researching cases for factual verification, and preparing interrogatories and estimates.

Postconviction and Corrections Law

Paralegal works with inmate who wishes to appeal conviction and helps to identify problems. Helps with all aspects of appeal, including writing administrative complaints and gathering relevant records.

Products Liability Law

Area involves government regulations, factual investigation, manufacturing, toxic tort litigation, technical knowledge, federal legislation. If interested in this specialty, see also *Environmental Law*.

Public Interest Law

All aspects of law concerning welfare of public at large, including health and environment and safety regulations, including manufacture of safe products.

Real Estate Law

Paralegal assists law firms, corporations and development companies in transactions involving land, houses, office buildings, condominiums, shopping malls, and so forth, with research on zoning regulations, title work, mortgage closings, checking compliance on all disclosure settlements, foreclosures, office management, and tax-exempt industrial development financing.

Sports Law

A relatively new field with few positions. Area includes all aspects of sports law, including safety regulations, sports injury, and contract issues with owners, managers, and players.

Tax Law

Paralegal compiles all data for preparation of tax returns (including corporate income, employer income, employer quarterly returns, franchises, partnerships, sales, personal property, individual income, estate, gift taxes): drafts extensions, maintains tax law library, and compiles supporting documents for returns.

Tort Law

Paralegal mainly provides litigation assistance in civil wrong that has injured someone, such as negligence, trespassing, defamation, strict liability, wrongful death, and, frequently, worker's compensation for on-the-job injuries.

Trademark Law

Paralegal researches documents, investigates, prepares foreign trademark applications, maintains files, responds to official government actions, and investigates trademark infringement. See also *Copyright Law*.

Transportation Law

All areas included in transporting of individuals delivery of products, carriers, and state and federal jurisdictions. Assignments may include such areas as violation of weight, product, or carrier transportation laws.

Travel Law

Work in areas of contracts between operators and suppliers, class action suits with transportation companies and travel agencies, and jurisdictions over travel suppliers.

Tribal Law

Paralegal assists in civil and criminal cases in which both parties are Native Americans. Drafts and files complaints, and presents written and oral appeals in tribal court of appeals.

Trusts, Estates, and Probate Law

Paralegal collects data, handles preliminary drafting of wills or trusts and investment analysis in estate planning. Manages office, assists in administering estate of decedent (including asset phase, accounting phase, and termination-distribution phase). Assists in general litigation, including preparing sample pleadings, doing legal research, preparing drafts of interrogatories, and notarizing documents.

Unemployment Insurance (Compensation) Law

Paralegal meets with clients, investigates and solicits affidavits from employers, handles time determinations, serves as informal advocate with both parties, represents clients before Unemployment Insurance hearing examiner. Counsels clients, presents petitions before legislative and administrative hearings, and addresses community groups.

Welfare Law

Paralegal holds preliminary interviews to explain welfare issues, meets with welfare departments, investigates and verifies information, and conducts hearings and follows up with hearing attorney. Assists attorney in gathering documents for appeal, files papers in court, and serves papers. Trains other paralegals and speaks to community organizations.

Worker's Compensation Law

Paralegal interviews claimants, collects data, drafts claims, requests hearings, and serves as a formal or informal advocate. Follows up to determine whether payment is in compliance with awards, monitors claims, and files statutory demand for proper payment, if necessary.

Training for a Specialty

Whatever setting or specialty appeals to you, remember that you will develop many of your skills on the job. To qualify for the job or area you wish to enter, experience and training will vary, depending upon the competition in the current job market, and the specific position. Basically, however, a thorough, intensive paralegal training program, including computer skills, is excellent preparation for an entry-level position in any area. Check the qualifications required for the specialty (for example, language requirements for an immigration specialist). Learning on the job may otherwise provide the additional training essential for any given position.

The personal characteristics that are requisite for any position are equally important. In addition to those qualities which are the earmarks of a successful candidate for any job in any field—reliability, commitment, diligence, etc.—the successful paralegal will have the competitive edge if he or she has strongly developed oral and written communication skills and can relate well to other people. Working with clients, handling research, and getting along with a wide variety of personality types, frequently under stressful conditions such as stringent deadlines or a heavy load of multiple tasks, demands qualities that cannot be learned in a classroom. They are the characteristics lawyers look for when selecting the best paralegal for the position. The ability to put things into perspective, keep a sense of humor, and maintain a balanced outlook on life are all characteristics of a mature person who has the determination to get the job done but can also be counted on to work under demanding conditions.

Other skills that have been developed in other jobs, whatever the field, can enhance a paralegal's opportunity to get a position and to perform effectively on the job. Think of the knowledge and expertise you have gained through your college education, if you have a degree or have attended college. Critical thinking skills can be developed in any academic course or any environment. A major or minor in any field may be the source of valuable, relevant skills that could make you an asset. If you do not have a college education, you may have developed other work skills, including business skills, organizational skills, computer skills, and foreign language skills; all these and more may prove to be an asset to a firm or particular attorney. *Every* position presents an opportunity for someone to develop specific skills as well as accomplishments.

In a later chapter on interviewing, there is a list of personal and professional skills most sought after by employers. Personal traits as well as professional skills are extremely important. Communicating effectively, getting along with others, setting priorities, managing time, solving problems, handling change, taking criticism, and working well without supervision are among the many attributes that will impress a potential employer. If you do not possess them, find ways to develop them in any current educational, volunteer or work setting.

Of course, it is a given that you have the professional qualifications for the job. Many are not fully aware, however, of the range of those qualifications. In the next chapter, you will discover those skills, interests, and talents you have developed (if you do not already recognize them) along with your achievements. Once you discover your assets, you must learn how to convey them to a potential employer.

Preliminary Self-Assessment

Self-assessment or self-inventory is an essential part of the job search. You must begin there so that you can focus on those skills in a resumé. In order to do that, you need to take time to look at yourself and see where you have been and where you want to go as a paralegal.

All of this preparation will help you to prepare for the final stage: interviewing for the job. When a potential employer asks you to "tell me something about yourself," you will be prepared to answer, because by that time, you will have thought about it very carefully.

You will also be able to understand what there is about *you* that will make you a good paralegal. By understanding how you are *personally* prepared to do that job, you are getting ready to face your job campaign with all the tools and information you need.

So let's start at the beginning of the process: with *you.*

In order for you to determine if this field is the right match for you, how carefully have you analyzed the profession as it relates to your own skills and interests? It would be helpful, therefore, if you posed some very pertinent questions to yourself:

■ What specific skills do you think paralegals need to possess?

_____

_____

_____

_____

■ Have you ever spoken with a paralegal? If so, what were your impressions about this profession?

_____

_____

_____

_____

■ What do you find to be the most appealing aspect of the profession?

_____

_____

_____

_____

■ What are your salary expectations in this field?

_____

_____

■ What interests you about this type of work?

_____

_____

_____

_____

■ Where can you see yourself going in this profession? In five years?

_____

_____

_____

_____

■ What are your greatest concerns or misgivings about entering the profession?

_____

_____

_____

_____

■ Do you see any obstacles? If so, how would you overcome them?

_____

_____

_____

_____

Preliminary Self-Assessment Exercise

As a final exercise before you begin your self-assessment in the following chapter, write a brief statement about why you want to become a paralegal and why you think you are qualified.

Remember: This is a preliminary exercise. Nevertheless, you will be starting to think of yourself as a professional, in very specific ways. Later on, after you have completed the self-assessment of your skills, you will be asked to do another version of this exercise. You may wish to return to this page to see how much you have learned about yourself in the pages that follow.

■ Why I would like to become a paralegal:

_____

_____

_____

_____

_____

_____

_____

_____

_____

3

Self-Assessment and Self-Inventory

The purpose of a self-assessment, which is frequently referred to as a self-inventory, is to help you focus on your qualifications, skills, and achievements, so that you can best present them to a potential employer in a resumé. In order to do this, however, you must carefully review all of the activities in which you have participated and all of the jobs you have held (part-time or full-time, paid or volunteer). Go back as far as you like, or as far as you can recall a job that seems to have offered you an opportunity to develop *specific skills* or achieve *noteworthy accomplishments.*

The charts you are about to complete will be useful as part of your resumé preparation. They will give you a broad view of your accomplishments as they relate to the work you have done, even though they do not represent your current field of interest.

List all the jobs you have held, even if the specific job was unpaid; the place of employment; and your title, duties, and accomplishments. Choose action words to record this information: administered, analyzed, coordinated, designed, developed, directed, established, evaluated, implemented, managed, organized, produced, promoted, researched, supervised, trained, wrote, and so forth. These words will remind you of specific skills you developed in what you did. That will later help you as you shape your resumé.

Begin with the most recent year you worked or held a job and proceed to list in reverse chronological order all the jobs you held, going back to the earliest job you can remember in which you developed any skills. At this point, don't be concerned with repetitious lines. You can edit the list later on.

In the "Accomplishments" column, describe what you feel are your most significant accomplishments or contributions to your jobs. These accomplishments should relate to specific areas, if possible, such as increased efficiency, better designs, higher sales or profits, improved human relations, better working conditions, new or improved programs, and happier or healthier work environments. And remember to use those action words as you list these accomplishments.

After a review, you may wish to add to this chart later on. At this point, try to write down as much information about yourself as you remember.

Analyzing Your Accomplishments and Evaluating Your Skills

Now that you have chronicled your activities, what you have enjoyed doing and seem to be doing consistently, either on a job or as an outside interest, let's examine how your achievements or accomplishments are related to what you enjoy doing and identify the network of specific skills you have developed over the years.

On the following pages, you are asked to identify your skills. After reviewing your chronology chart, you should have a fresh idea of what you did in your previous jobs and activities. Now you are given the opportunity to focus on these skills again as an essential part of your resumé preparation, and can indicate the degree of competence you feel that you have achieved. Although you may find some overlapping, you will discover trends and patterns in your life, along with specific skills you have developed.

After completing your work chronology draft and skills inventory, you will probably realize that skills do not exist in isolation. Any one skill involves a whole series of related and transferable skills. If you can realize how the things you do well are generally related to what you enjoy doing, then you have reached a very important stage in thinking about your career.

Here are some examples of how you can achieve such a realization.

Perhaps you are happiest when you work with people you know, but you are not comfortable with strangers. Perhaps you are happiest when you work alone. You may dislike the type of work you are doing, but love solving problems related to your job, whether they are financial or personal problems. You may relish situations in which you can be the organizer or person in charge. You may enjoy building a boat or cooking a gourmet meal, but not enjoy following a specified set of instructions. What should become obvious to you is what makes you happy while you are working or playing.

Common threads may not be apparent, and sometimes it is easier to work with someone—a spouse or friend—who can help you recognize the skills you have developed or that are transferable. Such an exercise can be extremely beneficial as you prepare your resumé or plan for your job interview.

Work Chronology

Year	Organization	Title	Duties/Activities	Skills/Accomplishments (Rate your enjoyment level: Enjoyed:+ or Did not enjoy:–)

Skills Inventory

Skill	Excellent	Very Good	Good	Fair	Skill	Excellent	Very Good	Good	Fair
Analyzing					Problem-solving				
Budgeting					Persuading				
Building					Policy-making				
Computer Skills					Promoting				
Specific Programs:					Researching				
					Repairing				
					Selling				
Coordinating					Shorthand				
Counseling					Supervising				
Creating					Speaking				
Decision-making					Teaching				
Designing					Training				
Directing					Troubleshooting				
Drafting					Typing				
Editing					Writing				
Inventing					Others:				
Languages (specify)									
Leading									
Listening									
Managing									
Meeting Planning									
Motivating									
Negotiating									
Observing									
Organizing									
Performing									
Planning									
Presenting									

Anything from organizing a car pool to managing an office requires a special skill. Skills required for a job may seem to be more valued (since you are paid to use those skills) than those used in a hobby, homemaking, or volunteer work, but *they may be the same skills.* A chairperson for a charity fund-raising drive has acquired skills in planning, organizing, delegating, bookkeeping, and communicating, as well as many others. A president of the Parents' Club at the local high school needs to develop skills in motivating others, promoting and publicizing, negotiating, writing and speaking, and dealing with people.

Almost anything you have done can be broken down into a series of steps and analyzed in terms of functions and skills. For example, you do volunteer work for a teenage rehabilitation center on weekends. You recognize that some of the teenagers have severe reading problems. You begin to read aloud to individual young people on a one-to-one basis, pronouncing and explaining the meaning of each word. What are you doing? You think you are helping a youngster, and you are, but let's analyze the situation a little more closely.

Problem: Difficulty in reading.

Reason: Youngster's lack of concentration and inability to recognize, understand, and pronounce words.

Solution: Build the youngster's self-confidence and attempt to understand his or her social and emotional environment. This takes patient, supervised practice and continued support as the youngster improves.

Once the situation is described, it becomes easier to identify skills you have developed and used, skills that may not be obvious at first glance. The help you give the youngster in the above situation involves the use of very specific skills. Helping the youngster to overcome a reading problem demonstrates an ability to perceive the core of a problem and offer a solution, and, in addition, you have demonstrated patience, understanding, and strong motivational and communication skills.

Any woman who runs a large household or has moved nine times in seven years has undeniable skills! Although she may not list those activities on her resumé, she must recognize that she does have strong managerial skills and will then come to perceive herself as capable of far more than the paid job experience listed on a resumé might otherwise indicate. Anyone who works on a school committee may have developed skills in buying, selling, motivating, negotiating, communicating, and many other areas. A person who has successfully raised funds has a business sense, an eye for detail and accuracy and a proven track record. Specific figures, such as dollar amounts in budgets or percentage increases, are evidence that can and should be included on a resumé.

A similar problem faces recent college graduates who have limited job experiences, including seasonal positions such as waitressing, bartending, retail selling, or clerical work.

How can you identify basic skills in these jobs without inflating their significance? Just think of those skills you have developed that would be useful in any profession and focus on them in your resumé.

For example: **Manager, The Back Door Restaurant**

- Worked varied shift schedules

- Supervised and trained temporary staff

- Handled cash receipts during vacation period for regular cashier

Retail Sales Clerk, Morton's Department Store

- Handled all cash sales in three departments

- Assisted in annual stock inventory

- Participated in employees' staff development program

Salad Chef, Jeremy's Cafe

- Worked rotated day and evening shifts

- Closed cafe and balanced daily cash receipts

- Maintained inventory chart

Secretary and Computer Clerical Worker, Manpower, Inc.

- Handled temporary assignments for area companies during holidays and summers

- Developed and used computer skills for updating and maintaining company files

- Served as receptionist and scheduled appointments

- Performed wide range of office duties as necessary, including typing, filing, photocopying, and packaging

The point here is that you cannot expect a potential employer to dig out these skills for you. You can do it once you recognize them. This is how the self-inventory chart can help you. Appreciate your past experiences and learn to articulate the skills you have found—both on your resumé and in an interview—rather than apologize for what you think you have not done!

On a job application, in an interview, or even in casual conversation, never use a negative approach such as "Although I do not have any specific experience in . . . ." Rather, focus on the skills you *have* developed in various settings that are appropriate and relevant to the job for which you are applying.

If you have been out of the job market or are entering an unrelated field, you must emphasize how you might have acquired strong skills in communication, management, interpersonal relations, or other areas from your past experience. Stress how these skills could be very useful in the particular position that is open.

When you are applying for a paralegal position, for example, focus on how your experience in *other* fields could prove to be an asset to you. Build on your achievements and experiences; make a potential employer recognize how much you have to offer, even though you have little or no experience in the position for which you are applying. You are more than qualified. Your job is to convince the person who will be hiring you. More strategies in "selling yourself" are discussed in a later chapter on interviewing. The **Interview Self-Evaluation Checklist** in Appendix B of this book will also be helpful as you progress to that stage.

When you realize all that you have achieved, your self-confidence will be greatly enhanced. Some of the gnawing questions will be answered: "I'm _____ years old and all I have done is teach . . . . or keep house . . . . or volunteer . . . or (fill in the blanks yourself), so who would want to hire me as a paralegal?"

When you begin to look at yourself in the most expansive way possible, it becomes easier to answer such a question in the most positive terms. That has been the purpose of this chapter on self-assessment.

Over these past few pages, you have been scrutinizing yourself, perhaps more carefully than you have ever done before. Doing so is essential if you are to successfully embark on your new career.

All of this self-discovery will lead to the results you want. When you become a paralegal, you've taken a bold new step into a field that requires a new set of skills, but employers hire an entire person, not just a set of skills. What makes you valuable, both as a potential employee and a human being, is your combination of interests and values, as well as your skills. Yet before you can convince an employer that you are the best person for the job, you must have a fairly clear idea of what you can offer. You must be realistic and honest, but at the same time, you must be able to present the best picture of yourself, including your strengths and achievements.

In the past several pages, you have been carefully evaluating yourself as a prospective employee. This has been some of the most important preliminary work of your job search, particularly as it relates to your resumé.

It has taken a great deal of probing and self-reflection to recognize what you have done. Now you are asked to review the information you have gathered about yourself and begin to find the phrases that capture what you have done. You may have already begun to choose and use some words that indicate the types of actions in which you were involved.

Words that describe your previous jobs, particularly job titles, may not be very helpful. However, words that convey accomplishment, involvement, or participation put your skills into focus. In analyzing your achievements, words or phrases such as "I was responsible for . . ." or "My duties involved . . ." do not convey what you actually did on the job.

A partial list of action words follows. It is important for you to be able to convey your own value to potential employers. Choosing the right words is essential if you are to convince them that you would be an asset. You may wish to use the following words or add to the list any words that are not included but may be appropriate for you. Be certain to include your computer skills as well as other specific skills you have to offer.

administered	drafted	invented	promoted
analyzed	edited	maintained	reduced costs
conducted	established	managed	researched
contracted	evaluated	operated	sold
created	exhibited	organized	supervised
designed	expended	planned	supported
developed	implemented	prepared	trained
directed	improved	produced	wrote

Review the list and select those words that describe skills you have developed in your previous jobs. You may wish to review your earlier exercises to help you.

If you are still having a difficult time, examine the following entries, which can serve as models for your own achievement analysis. These examples can be expanded upon. Notice the use of action verbs, the avoidance of job descriptions, and the specific details used to quantify or demonstrate how the skill was achieved.

Examples of Job Skills and Accomplishments

Job Experience (Paid or Unpaid)	Accomplishments
Hospital fundraiser	<ul><li>Helped to raise $500,000 for new hospital wing</li><li>Purchased equipment for handicapped children</li><li>Established outpatient counseling facility</li></ul>

- Coordinated annual fashion show, netting $75,000
- Developed computerized data bank for mailing list

Assistant food manager for non-profit produce outlet

- Purchased foods
- Determined price lists
- Recruited volunteer sales staff
- Kept monthly books
- Wrote and distributed monthly reports to co-op members using desktop publishing

Administrative assistant to state director of family counseling

- Coordinated program lecture series for community group
- Initiated and implemented volunteer crisis alert program
- Developed promotional media for child abuse prevention

Alumni committee member

- Planned and organized parent-student orientation for incoming new and transfer students
- Coordinated annual phonathon for alumni contributions
- Wrote alumni news column in quarterly newsletter

Executive secretary to president

- Edited annual company report
- Supervised office of 15 staff members
- Designed invitations and programs for "Meet Your Staff" luncheons
- Designed and developed executive microfilm library for international conference

---

Now it's your turn.

Review all the exercises you have completed in this chapter, and study the examples provided. Then, combine this information about yourself into a cohesive whole. Begin by listing your job experiences (as you did at the first stage). Along with these jobs, identify what you did—your achievements and accomplishments. Use action words that focus on these skills.

What you are doing is putting together a comprehensive profile of what you have to offer a potential employer. Your personality traits will also emerge. Perhaps you are a person who not only has multiple skills and talents but who also has patience, the ability to work with people, organizational and communication skills, and persistence and reliability.

If you have been out of the job market (in order to raise a family, for example) or have spent years in a career that seems far removed from the paralegal field, then it is your challenge to convince a potential employer that you possess valuable skills that only time and varied experiences can bring: problem-solving skills and decision-making abilities, as well as diligence and determination. What employer could ask for higher qualifications?

As you review these last pages and prepare the final exercise in this chapter, you will be reviewing your past and learning how to build on your experiences.

In this final exercise, you are asked to do a summation of your work history, focusing on the skills you wish to present in your resumé. You may want to review your first work chronology draft that you completed earlier in this chapter.

Be certain to be as specific as you can in the skills and accomplishments column, and remember that action verbs will illustrate what skills you were using. This information will become an important part of your resumé, the topic of the next chapter.

Summary of Skills and Qualifications

Skills

List the skills you have developed in your previous positions. Review what you have included on the last pages. You may also wish to review the previous chapter, in which you were asked to evaluate your level of competence in various skills. Focus on the *skill word* you will be using in your resumé.

_____

_____

_____

_____

Qualifications

How would summarize your qualifications? Again, review the last pages to determine what you have done in your previous jobs (paid and unpaid).

Work Chronology

Year	Organization	Title	Duties/Activities	Skills/Accomplishments

Try to include your most marketable qualifications in one sentence. You will find this a helpful exercise as you prepare your resumé.

_____

_____

_____

_____

Before you go on with your resumé preparation, you are asked to complete the following exercise which will help you to see yourself as a paralegal. It will require you to think of all the personal and professional qualifications you bring to the profession.

Why I think I am qualified to become a paralegal:

_____

_____

_____

_____

_____

_____

_____

4

The Resumé

A resumé is a word portrait, your *professional profile*, the profile that you want to show a prospective employer. It is not a complete picture, but it does include the highlights from your background, training, and experience that you wish to emphasize. Remember, you are in control of the words on paper, and how you shape your resumé can help an employer focus on the areas that you want to be recognized immediately.

Essentially, then, the resumé is your professional introduction, and while it cannot get you a job, it should help you to get an interview—and that is the purpose of the resumé.

In order to create a resumé that will present those qualifications you wish to stress, you will have to do a great deal of preliminary work before you get the finished product. In the previous chapter, you were asked to do this preliminary work. Now let's see how you can build upon it.

What you may have realized by this time is that there is no one right way to write a resumé; there is no one format that is best for everyone. However, there is a right way and a best format for you, one that will work in helping you to integrate the many aspects of your background as you proceed in your job search as a paralegal.

In Chapter 3, you thoroughly examined your training, education, and experience. The importance of such an intensive self-assessment was to help you recognize what you have to offer an employer. That chapter required you to summarize what every employer is looking for in a job candidate: *skills and accomplishments*. Keep those two words in mind. An employer wants to know why you are the best person for the job, based on what you can do (your skills) and the evidence that you have done it (your accomplishments).

Conveying those skills and accomplishments on paper may be achieved in a number of ways. Keep in mind, however, that you must clearly demonstrate that *you are the person to be called in for the interview because you are the best qualified person for the job*. As you examine each section of the resumé, you will learn how to shape your self-assessment information to be that person.

Before beginning, however, remember that everything on your resumé must be verifiable. In a competitive job market, it might be tempting to include a degree you did not earn, a prestigious school you did not attend, a more marketable major you do not have, or a particular job title you do not hold. Who will ever know?

Aside from the ethical considerations of including erroneous or misleading information, it is far too risky to do so. If the fraud is detected, you will be eliminated from the applicant list, or, if you have the job, you will most likely be fired. Your credibility will be lost. Even the unintentional printing error of an employment date has been known to keep an otherwise attractive job candidate from being hired.

The range and reasons for such embellished data on a resumé are wide. Many actually convince themselves that they *almost* have a degree and so they include it; others believe they performed the functions of a particular position and list a job title they felt they earned. The naive assumption is that an employer will not bother to check out the information. In an attempt to appear more qualified, such a person ultimately conveys a lack of honesty and integrity.

On the other hand, it is more likely that you will *not* give yourself credit for what you *have* achieved or developed. A closer examination of the previous chapter should help you as you prepare your resumé, whatever format you choose.

Format of the Resumé

The basic formats listed below are almost self-explanatory. Each has advantages and disadvantages. You can decide which is most appropriate for you once we have discussed each one and you have an opportunity to examine the sample resumés with various formats included at the end of this chapter.

The **chronological resumé** lists all education and work experience in reverse chronological order, from the present to the past.

The **functional** or **skills resumé** emphasizes experiences and how they relate to the job that the candidate is seeking. This format stresses skills and achievements without focusing on the specific dates and places, although they are included.

The **combination resumé** format blends the advantages of the chronological resumé with those of the functional resumé. It can be the most complete, the most general, and the most specific, all at the same time. But it must be coordinated skillfully to avoid the appearance of a hodgepodge of unrelated experiences.

For the purposes of your resumé as paralegal, it should be stressed that while you have some latitude in arranging your material and information, there are some guidelines that should prove very helpful. Let's look at each section as it should be considered.

Keep in mind an important point: Most employers prefer to receive a one-page resumé from entry-level paralegals. Later on in this chapter, we will discuss how you can make the best use of the margins, choice of paper, type styles, headings, and other details. You are still in a preliminary stage at this point, so it is far more essential that you write down everything you wish to include in your resumé and then see how you can combine areas or edit your information. It is far easier to edit later than to try to remember what you left out.

Resumé Categories

While the final order of your material will depend on the format you choose and the emphasis you wish to place on certain information, it will be helpful for you to identify major categories that you want to include. Each of these points is discussed in detail in the following pages, before you put together your final resumé. Some of them are optional, and others are essential.

Personal Information
Career Objective
Summary of Skills and Qualifications
Education
Work Experience
Professional Activities
Special Awards and Recognition
Military Experience
Special Interest and Community Activities
References

In order of appearance, let us now consider some essential items to be included in your resumé, regardless of the final format you choose.

Personal Information

Name   Address   Telephone Number

The above items are the *only* ones that you are required to provide by law. This information should be included at the top of your resumé where it will be readily seen.

Do not include the entry titles, such as *Name, Address,* and *Area Code* and *Telephone Number,* when you give this information. Do not list formal titles here or any nicknames. Such informality may demonstrate friendliness but not professionalism.

In your address, list the place where you can be contacted when you send out you. resumé. If you will have a different address after a specified date, you may list two addresses. For example:

430 South Wabash Ave. Apartment 202	(After December 15,1995) 127 St. Charles Court
Chicago, Illinois 60605	Miami, Florida 33161
(312) 341-3289	(305) 267-l806

Be sure to include a telephone number at which you are certain someone is available to answer calls. If you are listing an out-of-town number, explain in your cover letter that you will call the potential employer. As a job applicant, you should not expect a potential employer to pay the costs of a long-distance telephone call. Indicate the specific time you will call, and then do so. If you cannot be available to answer your phone, ask someone to do it for you, use an answering machine with a professional message, or arrange to use voice mail.

Do not list a work phone unless you have permission to do so or know for certain that it will not prove awkward for you to receive a phone call. Keep some important points in mind regarding telephone calls:

- Make certain that you have left a clear, direct message with a time that you will return your calls.

- It does not seem reasonable to ask someone to call after business hours.

- Avoid cute messages designed to impress your listener. They usually have the opposite effect. Remember that a potential employer may not wish to leave a message at all if *your* message is unprofessional.

- Do not expect a potential employer to make an unreasonable effort to contact you. There are many other willing and available job candidates.

Other pointers: Do not include photographs, or give your marital status or other family information. Other personal information that may reveal your age, health, or marital status is not relevant and could possibly keep you from getting to the interview stage. You do not know what personal bias a potential employer might have. You cannot be denied a job *legally* because of your age or young dependents, particularly if you are a woman, but your resumé may be rejected for any number of reasons. For example, one woman stated that she was a single parent of three children. She believed that such information would demonstrate that she could handle multiple responsibilities and could manage her time efficiently. A potential employer looked at that and saw a person who might be absent from work if emergencies arose with her family. Again, legally a person cannot be denied a position because of personal circumstances. However, you want to give yourself the best opportunity to get the interview. On the other hand, *do* include information that could make you more attractive for a specific job, such as willingness to relocate, if that is appropriate for you.

Career Objective

Many feel that stating a job or career objective on a resumé locks them into one specific area and that they should leave all their options open by writing a general resumé. Others feel that career objectives often sound too contrived, although that need not be so. A career objective *is* optional, but if you decide to include it, make it work for you.

Employers are looking for people with specific skills, and a brief career objective can indicate that you are a person who has a clear idea of where you are going. A career objective, therefore, could be helpful if it fulfills a purpose. It should focus on what you think you can and would like to do, based on your skills and qualifications. It need not be lengthy, but it should add something to your resumé; otherwise, omit the category. If you choose to include it, the examples below should be helpful.

- An entry-level paralegal position offering increasing responsibilities and opportunities in real estate or land development.

- A challenging paralegal position that would enable me to use my intensive generalist training and legal research skills, as well as my diverse academic and employment background.

- A challenging litigation paralegal position that will utilize my knowledge of computer database systems.

For additional examples, study the model resumés included at the end of this section.

Again, remember that the career objective is an optional entry. A vague, confusing, or redundant objective would only be a disadvantage for you.

Summary of Skills and Qualifications or Highlights

Although the category **Summary of Skills and Qualifications** is also optional, it can serve a useful function. It clearly focuses those skills and qualifications you have developed over the years, so that an employer can readily see how they relate to a paralegal position. It can also help you pull together various types of experiences you may have developed in several different types of jobs.

In the last chapter, in which you completed your self-assessment and self-inventory, you were asked to summarize the skills you had developed in your various positions, both full-time and part-time, paid and unpaid. You may wish to review that chapter and the final list in which you summarized your skills. You may want to revise the list or write a one- or two-sentence summary now.

The statement at the beginning of the resumé can help a potential employer immediately recognize what you have to offer as an employee.

The following examples may give you some idea of how to focus your own skills and qualifications in a summary statement.

> **Summary of Skills and Qualifications**: Extensive experience in varied settings has enabled me to develop strong communication skills, specifically research, writing, and verbal and interpersonal communication. My organizational and detail-oriented background should prove to be an asset in a paralegal position.

Highlights, as the term implies, point up your strongest, most marketable traits.

> **Highlights:** Strong organizational and communication skills, combined with intensive paralegal training and experience in varied legal and non-legal settings, have provided me with the necessary qualifications to perform at high-level capacity.

Review your own highlights and determine if they will attract the attention of an employer in a summary statement. If you decide to omit this entry, you should still review your qualifications, so that you can include your most marketable qualifications in your cover letter.

Education

The section on education is usually the first major category in a paralegal's resumé, particularly for an entry-level position, unless there is a reason to include it as the last category. (One of the sample resumés included does list the education category last.) For the most part, however, an employer will want to see your education, background, and training immediately. Describe your education, beginning with your paralegal training, where you received it, when you received it, and your specialty, if you had one. Not all programs have been approved by the American Bar Association. If your program does have ABA approval or if it is a graduate-level certificate program, be certain to include that information. If it is not ABA approved but follows ABA guidelines, you can include that. Depending on the space you have, you may wish to include specific courses or the number of hours of training. Be certain, however, that you do include the significant essential information that clearly indicates that you are a trained paralegal. The resumé samples that follow illustrate how you can list all of this information briefly but completely.

Review these resumé samples to determine how you wish to present your material. Use reverse chronological order, giving the most current information first and then working backward. Include important details such as the curriculum used (specialty or generalist program), computer training, or other relevant information you would like to emphasize.

If you have not attended college, make certain that you focus on your particular achievements in high school that reveal important qualifications. Did you participate in organizations that required specific skills such as thinking on your feet, communicating ideas, or expressing yourself with clarity and persuasiveness? Special projects (at school or within the community) or part-time jobs also demonstrate commitment, initiative, and responsibility.

If you attended college, include where you went, your degree (if you graduated) and your major and minor, if relevant. Avoid listing months and any other details that will clutter your resumé. *Do* include special awards or honors, as well as your grade point average if it reflects your academic achievement.

Should you include your graduate degree or graduate study? Or will this "overqualify" you for an entry-level position? Think of all the important skills and the overall background you have developed. The issue is how to include this information so that it becomes an advantage for you. If an employer feels that you will always be dissatisfied or leave when something better comes along, impressive qualifications could disqualify you.

Your job is to convince the employer that you are willing to begin at an entry-level position because you do *not* have skills and experience in this new field as a paralegal, and your graduate study (if you have any) will prove to be an asset to them and should help you to move ahead quickly. Be certain, however, that you believe this yourself before you attempt to convince anyone else.

Work Experience

This category may just as easily be entitled **Work History, Employment Record, Professional Experience**, or any other title that is descriptive of the employment information you are about to list.

In this section, it is important for you to tell where you worked, the dates (years), your title, and what you did on the job. Do not omit dates. Employers will want to verify where you worked and when. It is also essential for you to proofread your final resumé carefully for the accuracy of dates. A typographical error has actually cost some applicants the job! Do not distinguish part-time from full-time jobs, or paid from unpaid volunteer work. You may wish to group summer jobs or jobs held while in school that helped to finance your education. The completed resumés at the end of this chapter illustrate the widely varied ways in which you can include this information.

Most of the preparation for this category has already been completed in the previous chapter. Review that section, particularly the part in which you were asked to identify your skills by using action verbs.

Include all of your jobs, and indicate what skills you developed, skills that could strengthen you as a candidate for a paralegal position. If you have not had extensive job experience, you may include skills developed in your college activities or volunteer work. Internships may be included in this section if your work experience is limited; otherwise, you may include internships under the **Education** category.

If you wish to deemphasize dates of employment, particularly if you have been out of the job market for some years, you may wish to use a functional format, one in which skills are emphasized in clusters and dates are listed at the end of the resumé. Examine the resumé samples which use this format if you think it could be appropriate for you.

Other Categories

Other categories on your resumé may be optional. If you have special honors or awards, include them, so an employer can identify you as someone with unique talents and achievements. If you have been involved in community activities, a category may be included to indicate the level of responsibility and skills you have developed.

If you have military service, include it as a separate category.

If you have strong computer skills, technical skills, or special language proficiencies, be certain to include them.

Remember that your resumé is your professional profile, so think of the person who will be reading it. Does your resumé reflect what you have done and are capable of doing? Have you focused on your skills and accomplishments? That is what employers look for.

References

As your final entry, simply list the statement: References available upon request.

It is not appropriate to include a list of your references. You may be asked to include them on a job application, or in your cover letter you may include someone in the organization who knows you and has referred you to this position. It is also a good idea to take a list of references to the job interview and leave them with the interviewer, if it seems appropriate for you do do so. And remember, *always* ask your references for permission to use their names and indicate that they may be contacted. In Appendix B of this book, some guidelines on types of references you should use are listed, including appropriate choices and how you should present them in a separate reference list that you should prepare as part of your job search strategy.

The following guidelines summarize points for you to keep in mind as you develop your resumé. Study the resumé samples for further ideas.

Guidelines for Developing an Effective Resumé

Appearance of the Resumé

1. Choose high-quality bond paper (twenty-five pound rag content), in white, off-white, gray, or beige. The latter colors will offer distinction without distraction. If you choose these shades, use envelopes of a matching color.

2. With so many professional duplicating processes available today, it will not be difficult for you to choose one that will make your resumé take on the professional appearance you want. Many print shops will photocopy your resumé inexpensively. If you choose this process, be certain that the original typing is flawless and is completely camera ready. You may wish to have your resumé typeset and find that the cost is reasonable enough for you to make this investment. A reminder: Always proofread your printed copy before leaving the print shop. If you do not, any errors you later find will be corrected at your own expense.

   Laser printing is equally acceptable, and if you have access to a computer, you may find this process will provide many options, particularly if you want to revise or change details for various employers. You also have the advantage of choosing different sizes of lettering or boldface and italics for emphasis. However, take care not to overdo the use of these varied letter styles and prints. Attorneys who will be reading your resumé are very conservative.

Some final notes on the duplication of your resumé: Dot matrix computer copies are not suitable for final resumés. Never use poorly reproduced copies of your resumé. It also goes without saying that handwritten resumés (as well as cover letters and follow-up letters) are never acceptable, no matter how fine or elegant your handwriting.

3. Use the standard paper size of 8fi by 11 inches. The envelope may be regulation business size or a larger envelope that allows you to mail your resumé without folding it.

4. Whatever process you choose, your resumé should be error free. Remember that ultimately, you are responsible for any misspellings, typographical errors, or printer's errors.

5. Use capital letters sparingly. The same holds true for underlining. The purpose of these devices is to make words stand out. If they are overused, nothing will stand out. The sample resumés included in this book demonstrate the effective use of print format.

6. Do not abbreviate. All organizational names (for example, American Medical Association, American Management Association) should be spelled out. Degrees, special awards, and all titles should also be spelled out fully.

7. If the institutional or organizational name of a former employer has been changed, indicate the current name as well as the former name (for example, Midwest State University; Midwest Teachers College; or AMGRO, formerly American Textile Growth Corporation).

8. Be consistent in your layout and composition. Complete sentences will take up valuable space. If you decide to use phrases instead, be certain they are grammatically correct and free of ambiguity.

9. Use past tense for previous activities, experiences, or acquired skills. Present tense refers to ongoing or current activities.

10. Consult a dictionary for correct spellings. If you are a poor speller, have someone else proofread your final copy. It is also a good idea to have someone else proofread the final copy you receive from the printer, if at all possible.

11. Use white space for eye appeal and easy reading. Use ample margins, and make certain they are uniform. Use indentations and tabs to add white space and emphasize key points. If you have extensive information you want to include on your resumé, you may be tempted to cram in as much as possible onto one page. Doing so will use up the margins, as well as make the resumé difficult to read. You want an employer to be able to easily identify the skills and experiences that you have. One solution to this problem is to use a smaller print size in some categories. Typesetting or laser printing will enable you to do this easily.

12. Edit your resumé to make sure you include all the essential points, but avoid unnecessary details. Do not ramble on or include a philosophical

statement about yourself, your profession, or the world in general. If your employer wants to get to know you, you will be called in for an interview.

13. Use precise language. Avoid jargon. Do not use pompous or self-serving descriptions, such as *invaluable, highly creative, sensitive,* or *perceptive,* to describe yourself in your career objective or any other part of your resumé. Let your reader come to such conclusions based on what your credentials and accomplishments, as well as your references, say about you.

14. Constantly update your resumé. Never send an old resumé to which you have added recent items. If an important event such as the receipt of an honor or award occurs after your current resumé has been printed, you may include the specific item in your cover letter.

15. Your resumé will be a reflection of you—your style, as well as your history of professional accomplishments. Therefore, you should not allow anyone else to write it for you. Suggestions and comments from others are helpful insofar as they can improve what you say or what you omit. But your style and format should be as unique and individual as you are.

In the sample entries that follow, notice the use of action verbs to depict skills and achievements.

Sample Career Objectives

- Experienced paralegal seeks position using background in library science and legal research.

- Career objective is a challenging paralegal position involving coordinating, communicating, and researching, with opportunity for growth.

- Career objective is an entry-level paralegal position to use my experience in real estate sales and marketing, in combination with my training in legal research specializing in real estate.

Sample Highlights

- Professional paralegal will incorporate experience in patents and trademarks, anti-trust litigation, bankruptcy, and legal research. Supervisory and administrative background, combined with verbal and written communication skills.

- Professional paralegal specializing in corporate real estate acquisitions with proven results in developing innovative and cost-saving procedures.

- Extensive experience in legal environments has enabled me to develop communication skills (specifically, research and writing). Additional intensive training in a generalist curriculum has broadened the scope and depth of my understanding of the duties and responsibilities of a paralegal.

Sample Employment Descriptions

- Researched, compiled, and wrote corporate report documents.
- Developed methods and procedures to ensure efficient work flow.
- Supervised hiring and management of clerical and paralegal employees.
- Analyzed and reviewed preparation of tariff filings for submission to the Civil Aeronautics Board.
- Supervised and trained tellers.
- Balanced accounts of daily transactions.

Sample Community and Professional Activities

- Guest lecturer for Illinois Paralegal Association.
- Designed and presented salary negotiation seminar.
- Campaign coordinator: Managed all aspects of local drug awareness program for elementary and junior high school students, including issuing press releases, contacting speakers, and moderating panel.
- Volunteer for Chicago Literacy Foundation.

Sample Resumés

The following pages provide sample resumés. They illustrate different formats and techniques that have been discussed in this chapter. As you review these, note the differences between chronological resumés and functional or skills resumés.

A variety of formats have been included. Again, depending upon what you wish to emphasize, one format may be more appropriate than another. For example, although most employers prefer to see education as the initial entry, you may wish to emphasize your strong experience over your education. Check with your local paralegal program or association to determine if attorneys in your area have expressed a preference.

The organization of your material may also change based on your career advances. For that reason, several different types and formats are presented. Always keep in mind the position for which you are applying. Study the qualifications they are looking for, and make them easy to identify in your resumé. This may require changing your resumé for different positions to focus on specific, relevant details in your background and experience. It it is not difficult to make these changes, and it will be well worth your time and effort to do so.

Chronological Resumé: Legal Secretary

Mary Sue O'Brien
360 Greenleaf Road
Northfield, Illinois 60048
(708) 541-5678

OBJECTIVE: A paralegal or administrative position utilizing my legal assistant background and client relation skills.

EDUCATION:
1993-1995 **HARPER COLLEGE**, Palatine, Illinois
Associate Degree, Legal Technology Program

1995 **INTERNSHIP, Office of the County Clerk**
DuPage County Courthouse, Wheaton, Illinois

EXPERIENCE:
1991-1993 **LEGAL SECRETARY**
John A. Looby, Attorney at Law, Evanston, Illinois
Drafted and prepared wills; trusts; probate documents; individual, fiduciary, and estate tax returns; and real estate closing documents. Telephone and written correspondence, bookkeeping, billing, payroll, and office reception.

1990-1991 **CUSTOMER SERVICE REPRESENTATIVE**
Ravinia Festival Association, Highland Park, Illinois
Answered inquiries, accepted ticket orders, and resolved complaints of contributors and general public. Assisted with general office and accounting duties and implemented sales projects for management.

INTERESTS and Swimming, tennis, music.
ACTIVITIES: Community Recycling, Central DuPage Hospital volunteer, Citizens for a Better Environment.

HONORS and National Honor Society, Debating Team State Championship,
AWARDS: Senior Leadership Award, Junior Achievement Award.

REFERENCES: Furnished upon request.

Chronological Resumé: Insurance and Military Background

Carl Anderson
6345 College Oak Drive
Sacramento, California 95481
(714) 662-5565

Education

California State University
Los Angeles, California, 1993-1995
Certificate Program for Paralegals, Corporate Track

Sacramento High School Diploma, 1988

**Employment
History**

The Banker's Life, Fresno, California, 1993
Special Agent.

Designed and marketed insurance-related aspects
of employee benefits plan.

The Metropolitan Life, Hayward, California, 1992
Sales Representative.

Prepared and marketed multiline insurance and financial
programs to individuals and groups.

Navistar (formerly International Harvester),
Hayward, California, 1991-1992 *Quality Analyst.*

Managed material inventory and distribution.
Performed wide range of operations in
product quality and planning.

**Military
Service**

United States Army, 1988-1991
Communication Specialist: AFVN Radio and TV Saigon.

Wrote, produced, and reported news, music, and
promotional segments. Awarded Army Commendation
Medal. Honorable Discharge.

**Community
Affairs**

President, Blackhawk Homeowners' Association
Organized 5,000 homeowners to gain passage of water
quality legislation through California General Assembly.

References and writing samples available upon request.

Chronological Resumé: Real Estate Management

Helen Adams
2674 Bay Area Boulevard
Houston, Texas 60187
(713) 964-5588

EDUCATION

1995	Center for the Advancement of Legal Studies Houston, Texas Certificate of Completion
1988	Houston Bay High School, Diploma with Honors

WORK EXPERIENCE

1991-1994	Office Manager Top Realty, Houston, Texas Researched and selected prospective customers for potential sale of property; served as liaison to customer agent; handled customer service replies. Managed day-to-day office operations.
1989-1991	Secretary and Administrative Assistant Texas Board of Realtors, Houston, Texas Handled board inquiries and complaints, scheduled meetings with realtor representatives, and assisted in conference planning and program implementation.
1988-1989	Receptionist, Remax Real Estate Group Greeted clients, answered telephones, scheduled appointments.

SKILLS AND INTERESTS Computer programming experience: FORTRAN, COBOL. Travel, music, church council news editor.

REFERENCE Available upon request.

Chronological Resumé: Insurance and Sales Background

Allison Parker
7000 Roswell Road North East
Atlanta, Georgia 30328

(404) 742-8812

OBJECTIVE   A responsible paralegal position that will enable me to use my
professional training, business background, and language skills.

EDUCATION

1994   The National Center for Paralegal Training
Atlanta, Georgia
Generalist Program

Intensive training in civil and criminal litigation, real estate,
corporations, estates, trusts and wills, debtor-creditor relationships, family law, legal research, and computer literacy.

1988   Florida State University, Tallahassee
Bachelor of Arts, *cum laude*
Major: Business   Minors: Psychology, Spanish

EMPLOYMENT

1990 -1993   Voyager Financial Services, Jacksonville, Florida
Brokerage Technician for insurance company's leading brokers.

Processed insurance and investment product applications.
Provided services for existing accounts.

1987-1989   Broward & Barnett, Jacksonville, Florida
Sales Manager

Supervised sales agents, and estate and tax planning
specialists in creation of financial planning reports for clients.
Analyzed clients' assets, and prepared materials for computer
illustrations and word processing and management reports.

COMMUNITY ACTIVITIES

Adult Literacy Program in the Hispanic Community;
Sigma Theta Honor Society, Scholarship Chairperson;
Organist, Jacksonville Community Bible Church.

References available upon request.

Chronological Resumé: Education and Business Background

Ruth Martin
176 South Street
Garden City, New York 11530
(516) 667-3729

CAREER OBJECTIVE

A challenging position that would enable me to use my intensive generalist paralegal training, and diverse academic and employment background.

EDUCATION

1994

Adelphi University, Huntington, New York
Lawyer's Assistant Program
Generalist Curriculum. ABA Approved. Graduate level certificate.

1991

Syracuse University, Syracuse, New York
Bachelor of Science in Education

Junior academic year in Switzerland.
Special studies in educational theory and practice.

EMPLOYMENT

1991-1994

Board of Education of New York City, Brooklyn, New York
Member, Planning Team for Curriculum Reorganization
Conducted research for educational planning; implemented and evaluated pilot programs for six-school system.
Supervised student teachers, served as master teacher.

1987-1991

Various retail sales and clerical positions held to finance 80% of college education.

1989-1991

Proof Operator. Marine Midland Bank, Syracuse, New York
Encoded checks for Workmen's Compensation Fund accounts.
Developed debit and credit accuracy check system.
Trained new operators to work on specialized projects.

1985-1989

Library Assistant, Syracuse University, Syracuse, New York
Worked with collection and acquisition librarian.
Maintained periodical files.

INTERESTS

Photography; Member of Conservation Club; Volunteer for Teen Drug and Alcohol Rehabilitation Center.

References Available Upon Request.

Skills Resumé: Business and Sales Background

Anne M. Smith
1021 Wynwood Drive
Grand Rapids, Michigan 49501
(616) 637-3233

OBJECTIVE: A paralegal position to utilize my strong business skills and paralegal training.

EDUCATION: Certificate in Paralegal Studies, 1994
American Institute for Paralegal Studies, Inc.
Southfield, Michigan

Associate of Arts, Central Florida Community College,
Ocala, Florida, 1993

Legal studies highlights: Drafted complaints, answers, interrogatories, summons. Interpreted case and statutory law. Prepared court briefs and memoranda. Drafted, and filed court documents. Performed extensive legal research, case citing, and shephardizing. Emphasis on writing, litigation, pleadings, arbitration, business law, jurisprudence.

PROFESSIONAL SKILLS

Administrative Skills

- Performed general administrative and clerical duties.
- Handled petty cash, banking, payroll, accounts payable.
- Set up computerized office system.

Communication Skills

- Inventoried, displayed, sold merchandise.
- Managed sales department during peak periods.
- Assisted with promotion campaign and designed brochure.

Specialized Skills

- WordPerfect 6.0, 7.0, 7.5; Lotus 1-2-3; R Base Computer.

EMPLOYMENT: 1992-1993   United Distributors, Inc.
1991-1992   Anderson Professional Dental, Inc.
1990-1991   Foster-Brown Shoe Company

REFERENCES: Available upon request.

Skills Resumé: Teacher

SUSAN G. STONE

718 Franklin Road
Huntington, West Virginia 23219
(804) 863-5566

(After August 15, 1995)
P.O. Box 1041
Miami, Florida 33161
(305) 267-4327

EDUCATION

1994   **Pensacola Junior College**, Pensacola, Florida
Legal Studies: Civil and Criminal Litigation; Corporate
Law, Estate, Probate

1989   **Marshall University**, Huntington, West Virginia
Bachelor of Arts in Education

EXPERIENCE

Administrative and Management

Organized student government programs and activities.
Managed student governmental fundraising and
supervised disbursements.
Coordinated teachers' efforts to implement mathematics
pilot program.
Maintained inventory system for social science texts.
Assisted customers with problems and requests.

Communication

Completed classroom assignments in legal
writing, including briefing cases, drafting legal
documents, writing memos.
Researched, wrote, implemented multilevel instructional
units.
Designed and completed independent study projects.
Developed interpersonal skills through retail sales.

Teaching

Instructed adults in workshops and in-service training.
Taught 7th and 8th graders in student government classes.

EMPLOYMENT

1993-1994   B. Dalton Bookstore, Pineville, West Virginia Retail Sales
1989-1992   Wilson Elementary School, Sanford, West Virginia. Teacher
1985-1989   Summer and seasonal jobs in sales and waitressing to help
finance college education.

References   Furnished upon request

Skills Resumé: Diverse Background

Michael Johnson
1822 North Walnut Street
Flushing, New York 11366
(212) 442-5699

Education

1995   Nassau Community College, Garden City, New York
Associate Degree, Paralegal Program

1992   Computer Training Program, Westphal Training Center
Westphal, New York

1989   Davis High School, Diploma with Honors Westphal, New York

Skills   <u>Communication Skills</u>

- Edited newsletter for technology sales organization
- Conducted interviews for expanding staff
- Assisted in compiling index for monthly periodical

<u>Technical Skills</u>

- Researched and developed plant operation manuals
- Used research aids and wrote legal memoranda

<u>Organizational Skills</u>

- Coordinated work schedules at various plant sites
- Established daily operating procedures
- Supervised seven operators and mechanics

Work Experience

- Assistant Editor, *Techno-Info Monthly*,
  New Rochelle, New York, 1993-1995
- Division Coordinator, Power and Fuels
  Department, Inland Steel, East Chicago,
  Indiana, 1991-1993
- Staff Writer, *Citizens Perspective*,
  Flushing, New York, 1989-1990
- Editor, *Davis Views*, Davis High School publication, 1987-1989

Interests

Photography, swimming, science fiction

References available upon request.

Skills Resumé: Theater Background

Paul Jones
2020 North Harding Avenue
Chicago, Illinois 60623
(312) 927-7531

PROFESSIONAL
OBJECTIVE: A challenging position in a legal environment that will enable me to use my
extensive verbal, interpersonal and research communication skills as a paralegal.

EDUCATION
1995   Roosevelt University, Chicago, Illinois
Lawyer's Assistant Program: Certificate
Graduate Level ABA Approved Curriculum
Litigation, Legal Research, Computer Literacy

1990   Art Institute of Chicago and Goodman Theater
Bachelor of Fine Arts in Technical Direction

EXPERIENCE Communication
- University Instructor in Technical Direction
- Worked with staff from varied socioeconomic and educational
  backgrounds
- Created and implemented computer system for internal merchandise flow

Management and Supervision
- Supervised and coordinated crews of 10-150 persons
- Directed and executed cost estimating and purchasing of tools, equipment,
  materials
- Supervised year-round operation of all studios

Design
- Designed and renovated three-story building for film and television
  studio
- Designed over 195 theatrical productions

Technical
- Operations Coordinator and Designer
- Technical Director and Set and Lighting Designer
- Film and Special Effects Director
- Proficient in reading, drafting, and designing blueprints

EMPLOYMENT
1988-1994   Operations Designer, William Harrison Studios
1984-1988   Foreman, Stage Manager, Northwestern University
1980-1984   Technical Director and Designer, Florida State University
1978-1980   Instructor, Indiana University

REFERENCES Available upon request.

Margaret Garland
294 Green Street
Madison, New Jersey 07940

PROFESSIONAL
OBJECTIVE   A challenging position that would enable me to use my strong
interpersonal communication skills and paralegal training.

EDUCATION

1995   Hilbert College, Hamburg, New York
Bachelor of Science in Paralegal Studies
General Practice Curriculum: Corporations, Litigation, Real Estate
and Mortgages, Estates, Trusts and Wills, Criminal Law, Legal
Research

EXPERIENCE

COMMUNICATION SKILLS
- Worked with clientele from diverse backgrounds
- Provided customer assistance and information
- Contacted suppliers by telephone and letter

NEGOTIATION SKILLS
- Arranged for and executed purchasing of materials
- Established inventory priority list and arranged for deliveries

ORGANIZATIONAL SKILLS
- Assisted in planning presentation of stock items
- Assisted in compiling and computerizing inventory reports
- Implemented filing system to follow up on orders

EMPLOYMENT

1986 - Present   Child care and homemaker

1989 - 1991   Cashier and Baker, Parker Foods, Valley Stream, New York

1984 - 1986   Traffic Engineer, Village of Morton Park, New York

1982 - 1984   Social Work Intern, Herrick House, Queens, New York

REFERENCES Available upon request

Combination Chronological and Skills Resumé

Lydia Parker
2525 Tucson Boulevard
Tucson, Arizona 85705
(605) 795-1269

Objective: ***Corporate track paralegal position***

INTERNSHIP	Jamison, Jones and Carter, Tucson, Arizona

- Drafted resolutions, merger documents, and other corporate documents
- Maintained corporate minute books and stock ledgers
- Filed annual reports for domestic and foreign corporations
- Researched procedures of states regulating security sales

EDUCATION   Pima Community College, Tucson, Arizona
Associate of Applied Science Degree in Legal Assistant Studies, 1995

American Bar Association approved program

Concentration: Corporate Law
Courses: Paralegal Ethics, Corporations, Legal Research, Personal Injury, Bankruptcy, Commercial Transactions, Legal Writing

EMPLOYMENT   *Southwest Courier,* Tempe, Arizona
Feature and Opinion Page staff writer, 1992-1994
J.C. Penney, Customer Service and Sales, Phoenix, Arizona
Summer, 1992
Allstate Claims Adjustor, Tucson, Arizona, 1990-1992

SKILLS   Computer: WordPerfect 6.0, 7.0, 7.5, Lotus 1-2-3, dBase III+, DOS

Communication:

- Led student council annual community food drive
- Handled complaints through customer service
- Filed and handled accident and injury insurance claims
- Developed article leads and wrote newspaper features

INTERESTS and ACTIVITIES   Pima Community College Council: Chair, Executive Board
Tucson Association of Legal Assistants: Associate Member

References and Writing Samples Available Upon Request

Combination Chronological and Skills Resumé

Lisa Lewis
2190 Beulah Road
Glenview, Illinois 60025
(708) 998-1325

Objective: Paralegal position in personal injury law

EDUCATION
Institute for Paralegal Studies, Loyola University Chicago
Chicago, Illinois
Certificate in Paralegal Studies, December 1995
American Bar Association Approved Program
Courses included Personal Injury, Paralegal Ethics, Legal
Research (including Westlaw and Lexis), Commercial
Transactions, Legal Writing

Western Illinois University
Macomb, Illinois
Bachelor of Arts in Political Science, May 1995
Pi Sigma Alpha: Political Science Honorary Society

INTERNSHIP
Coffield, Ungaretti and Harris, Chicago, Illinois, Summer 1994
- Assisted in subpoena preparation
- Filed annual reports and court documents
- Maintained minute books and stock ledgers
- Scheduled and assisted attorneys in depositions

EMPLOYMENT
State Farm Insurance Company, Claims Adjuster, Elmhurst,
Illinois, 1990 - 1992
- Handled all aspects of injury claims files, including
scheduling appointments, and working with individual clients,
and submitting reports.

Nordstrom, Customer Service and Sales, Oakbrook, Illinois,
Summer 1992
- Worked with customers in successful resolution of complaints
- Followed up on actions taken to resolve problems and
complaints

Western Illinois University, Resident Counselor, 1993 - 1995
- Developed campus security awareness discussion forum
- Counseled resident students on academic and personal issues

INTERESTS and ACTIVITIES
Panhellenic Council; Chair, Executive Board
Illinois Paralegal Association: Associate Member
Volunteer: Central DuPage Hospital, DuPage Crisis Hotline

References and Writing Samples Available Upon Request

Chronological and Skills Resumé
Diverse background with legal procedures experience

Robert Altmeyer
1505 Lakeview Drive
Orlando, Florida 32856
(407) 843 - 2410

Professional Experience

- Williams Bay Legal Associates
Legal Procedures Assistant, 1990-1993

  - Filed legal documents
  - Assisted in closings and court appeals
  - Worked with attorneys in scheduling depositions
  - Researched and prepared proceedings

  Office Manager, 1990-1992

  - Handled accounts receivable
  - Developed office procedures manual
  - Trained clerical staff in computer programs
  - Planned and scheduled client and attorney meetings

  Century Commercial Real Estate Corporation, Orlando, Florida
  Administrative Assistant, 1988-1990

  - Researched and compiled market data on all commercial properties
  - Trained temporary personnel in office procedures
  - Compiled research data for company attorneys on legal issues
  - Scheduled closings on real estate sales
  - Supervised receptionist and clerical staff

Computer Skills: Proficient in WordPerfect 7.5, IBM Dos, Windows
Experience with Lexis and Westlaw

Community Activities South Orange Community Shelter Volunteer
Food Pantry Disaster Work Team

Professional Memberships: Member, Orlando Legal Assistants

Education: Bachelor of Arts in Legal Studies, University of Central Florida
Orlando, Florida
Graduated with honors, May 1995

Certificate of Completion: Computer Facility Training Program
Orlando, Florida
Summer 1994

References available upon request.

Final Checklist for Resumé Categories and Information

❐ Name
❐ Address
❐ Telephone number
❐ Career Objective (optional)
❐ Highlights or Summary of Skills and Qualifications (optional)

❐ *Education:*
  ❐ Schools
  ❐ Years
  ❐ Certificates
  ❐ Degrees
  ❐ Major Course of Study
  ❐ Specialized Training
  ❐ Honors (grade point average, if appropriate)
  ❐ Internships
  ❐ Special Activities and Projects

❐ *Employment:*
  ❐ Years
  ❐ Job Title
  ❐ Employer and Locale
  ❐ Job Responsibilities and Skills Developed
  ❐ Major Accomplishments
  ❐ Promotions

❐ *Professional Activities*
  ❐ Active Memberships and Title of Organizations
  ❐ Offices Held and Involvements
  ❐ Major Accomplishments

❐ *Community (Volunteer) Activities:*
  ❐ Titles of Organizations and Programs
  ❐ Specific Participation (Involvement, Offices Held)
  ❐ Major Accomplishments

❐ *Special Skills: Foreign Languages, Technical Skills, Computer Skills, and Other Skills*

❐ *Military Service*

❐ *Interests*

❐ *Other Relevant Information: Willingness to relocate, etc.*

❐ *References: Available upon request.*

5
The Cover Letter

Whether you are applying for a job that is listed in the want ads or any other place, including blind ads, your best chance for recognition will be the result of a clear, direct cover letter attached to your resumé. A good cover letter is well focused and specifically tailored to the job for which you are applying. While you probably have a standard resumé that you will include for all job applications, even in your mailing campaigns, every cover letter should be individual. To make this task easier, there are basic guidelines that apply to all the cover letters you write.

As a preliminary step to writing the cover letter, it should be helpful for you to think about the purpose of the letter: Who will be reading it? What do you want to achieve? How can you best do that? What will make your letter stand out from your competition so that the reader will see you as someone who has all the personal and professional qualifications he or she wants.

First of all, one of the basic rules of effective writing is to *know your audience.* This rule applies to writing cover letters. Will you be writing to a personnel manager? A paralegal manager? An attorney? Sometimes you can find out this information from the advertisement. If a name is given, you can call the firm and ask for that person's job title. If a name is not given but a firm is listed, you can call and simply ask who will be reading the applications. Once you have that piece of information, you can tailor your remarks to what you think that person might be looking for in a candidate.

As part of your preparation, you can find out which attorneys you will be working for: the number of attorneys, their specialities, even their backgrounds, if that information is available.

All of this information will help to shape the facts you include in your letter. For example, if the position is one that reports to three attorneys, it would be important to emphasize your skills and experience in working in such a situation or in being able to handle multiple responsibilities, work with minimal supervision, manage your time, and set priorities when organizing your tasks. If this information is available, you will position yourself nizing your tasks. If this information is available, you will position yourself at an advantage by including relevant details about yourself.

There are other ways in which information about the position as well as the reader of your letter will help you: What is there about the firm that appeals to you? What is there about your background, skills, and interests that would make you an asset to the firm?

Your letter is an opportunity for you to highlight your specific qualifications. Do you have exceptional writing skills? Have you achieved distinction in any area that would make you stand out as a candidate, in a work, volunteer, or school situation? You can do this very tactfully by highlighting information that is contained in your resumé.

Review your lists of accomplishments as well as your resumé. You may find just the right piece of information to include in your cover letter.

Basic Guidelines for Writing a Cover Letter

The following guidelines will help you as you prepare this important part of your job campaign.

1. If possible, find out the name of the person to whom you will be writing.

2. Who reads the letters of application? Will that person also be handling the interviews? The first person may screen the letters. You will want to be in the final group of candidates that are called in for an interview. Writing to that person by name will make a greater impression, if that information is available. Later on, if you are called in for an interview, you can do research on who will be interviewing you.

3. If the company is listed in the phone book, you can usually call and request information. What if only a post office box number is listed? There are varying views on how to address such a letter. All of them leave a great deal to be desired.

   "Dear Box 203A," "To Whom It May Concern," "Gentlemen," and "Madam" are considered to be the least preferable. "Dear Sir" has fallen into the sexist language category, and it might work against you, particularly if the interviewer happens to be a woman.

   Some appropriate suggestions included "Dear Personnel Manager" or "Dear Corporate Law Firm," if you wish to be conservative but still remain professional. You may also eliminate the salutation completely or simply address the letter to "Dear Sir or Madam."

Let good taste always be your guide, but if at all possible, find out the name of the person who will be reading your letter.

4. Demonstrate that you understand the requirements of the position and that you have the credentials as well as personal and professional qualifications to fulfill those requirements.

5. Include examples of specific results you have obtained that are relevant to the job. Reviewing your resumé and work chronology charts will be helpful.

6. Focus on key points of your resumé that emphasize your capabilities and experience.

7. Avoid any negative or apologetic remarks concerning qualifications you do *not* have for the job.

8. Be confident and positive about the qualities you do have, without sounding arrogant or boastful.

9. Emphasize how you can meet an important need of the company.

10. Do not ramble on or include any personal philosophical statements. Your letter should stand independent of your resumé. It must be to the point and directly related to the job. It should motivate the reader to read your resumé more carefully.

11. Keep your letter to one page in length. You will have time to expand your remarks and impress your interviewer in person. If that person is bored by a letter that is too long, you may never get to the interview stage.

12. Proofread your final letter carefully. Typographical errors, misspellings, or grammatical errors may cost you an interview.

13. Handle follow-up contacts with care and tact. A tactful follow-up call is permissible to see if your letter and resumé have arrived. You may also request an opportunity for an interview; if that is not possible, you may ask when interview selections will be made. After that, you must be careful not to alienate a potential employer or interviewer by any kind of abrasiveness. The line between confidence and brashness can easily be crossed. Sometimes it will depend upon the employer. One may ask that you not call for an appointment; another may find it a sign of initiative on the part of the job candidate. You must learn to read the signals. After making your initial call to see if your letter arrived, you must listen to the response to see if further action on your part is warranted.

Slightly different strategies should be used for the interviewing stage. Those strategies will be discussed later.

The Content and Form of Your Cover Letter

The order of your remarks in your cover letter should be straightforward. The following format may be a helpful guide.

1. *Opening. Capture the reader's interest.* Indicate where and how you found out about the job. If it was a newspaper ad, include the name and date of the paper, and the specific job for which you are applying. Some firms or organizations place several ads for different jobs in the same edition of the newspaper. If a mutual acquaintance referred you, be sure to include the name of the person. Also include a sentence or two about why you believe you could be an asset to the company.

2. *Middle. Make the reader want to meet you.* You can do this by demonstrating how specific achievements or results make you uniquely qualified for the job. You can refer to some part of your resumé or allude to a particular award or recognition you have received in the field. You may stress how a particular experience has provided you with useful insights into the field or job. It is also appropriate to refer specifically to the company's goals and objectives and how you could help meet them if you were hired.

   This section is particularly important for those who feel that they do not have the specific (or preferred) qualifications stated in the ad, but can bring other positive qualities to the job. It is also an opportunity for those who have been out of the job market for some time or who are changing careers to emphasize what they can bring to the job from their own background and professional experiences. Remember, volunteer work should not be distinguished from paid employment. Your skills and achievements should be the focal point.

3. *Ending: Stimulate the reader to action.* Request a personal interview, but leave the door open for you to make the call for an appointment, unless it is specifically stated that such calls will not be accepted. For example, you can end your letter by letter by saying "I look forward to discussing this position with you further and will call your office in a few days to request an appointment, if that is convenient for you." You must be alert to signals that would discourage you from calling or make make you appear abrasive. You can usually sense what would be appropriate when you call to ask for an interview or if you call ahead of time to get a specific name.

You will, of course, want to add your own individual style to your letter, but some of the guidelines given above should help you set the tone of your letter, and offer a direction to follow.

The cover letter often can be the deciding point on who is selected for the interview. And like any other part of your job search strategy, how well you are prepared in getting the job is every bit as important as how well you are prepared for the job itself.

Now examine the sample cover letters included. Notice how they have enabled the various applicants to tailor their specific qualifications to a job. Also notice the skill involved in pulling out those achievements and credentials directly related to the job.

Think about your own specific assets and how you can best relate them in your own cover letters. Doing so can help you convince a potential employer that you could very well be the best person for the job.

When setting up informational interviews, you should also follow these guidelines. This type of letter is one you will send out as part of a mailing campaign. A sample letter is included in this chapter.

How To Write a Persuasive Cover Letter: Do's and Don'ts

Do's

1. Discover your unique strengths that could prove to be an asset to this particular employer.

2. Focus on the specific achievements or skills you have developed in a recent job or situation (you may find these on your resumé), and highlight them in your letter.

3. Emphasize the positive qualities and relevant experiences you bring to this job—*not* what you don't have.

4. Read the job ad *very carefully*. What are they looking for? Take note of the specific language used. How do they list the requirements, preferred or essential? If they are looking for someone with specific skills, be certain to mention, in the exact same language, what you have to offer them. Doing so will let them see how exactly right you are for the job!

5. Close your letter with an action statement: How do you plan to follow up? Let your reader know when you plan to call, and then follow through with your plan.

6. Keep your cover letter to one page, with well-spaced paragraphs for easier reading.

7. Proofread your letter carefully and be certain to spell names correctly and give the proper titles and degrees, if appropriate.

8. Choose high-quality paper to reflect a polished, professional image. Remember: This letter is your introduction on paper. Use paper and envelopes that match the paper used in your resumé, if at all possible.

Don'ts

1. Do not cross the line from being confident to being overbearing. Let the tone of your letter indicate that both you and the company would mutually benefit from what you have to offer, not that this is a great career step for you.

2. Avoid language that describes you in self-congratulatory terms. Words such as *creative, perceptive,* or *outstanding* sound ego-inflating. Let others use those words in describing you. However, words such as *energetic, detail-oriented, organized,* or *disciplined* emphasize work-related qualifications and could be very effective in your letter, if they truly describe you.

3. Avoid any statements about the field or why you entered it. You may have an opportunity to talk about this in an interview. On the other hand, you may emphasize that the job offers you an opportunity to build on skills and achievements from the past, even in a different field.

4. Avoid graphics, colored paper, or anything that would cause your application to stand out in a negative way. Remember that this is a conservative profession.

Study the sample cover letters on the following pages to help you as your plan your own letters.

Sample Cover letter for Real Estates or Mortgages position.

2345 North Lake Street
Chicago, Illinois 60637
June 7, 1995

Ms. Marierose Alcocer
Midwest Realty Corporation
1822 West Madison Street
Chicago, Illinois 60607

Dear Ms. Alcocer:

Gary Adelman of your Finance Department has informed me of a paralegal
opening in your corporation. He believes that my background and training qualify me
for this position and has suggested that I apply.

As a recent graduate of Roosevelt University's Lawyer's Assistant Program with a
specialty in Real Estates and Mortgages, I have strongly developed skills in this particular
area. In addition, I have had practical experience in working with a small realty firm,
performing a wide variety of duties, including drafting financing documents, and
landlord and tenant agreements and working with attorneys in handling closings,
transferring deeds, and performing other related duties. Such training and experience
could make me an asset to your firm.

I will call your office within the next week to set up an appointment to discuss this
position at a time that would be convenient to you.

Thank you for your interest and consideration. I look forward to meeting you.

Sincerely yours,

Jean Pevan

125 Crescent Drive
Pittsburgh, Pennsylvania 15235
April 25, 1995

Mr. Michael Hiton
Cooley, Carson and Hall
225 Fifth Avenue
Pittsburgh, Pennsylvania 15209

Dear Mr. Hiton:

As one of the city's largest law firms specializing in litigation, Cooley, Carson and Hall can assuredly use the services of a paralegal with an excellent academic record and strong communication skills.

Recently, I received my Associate Degree in Applied Science from Erie Community College, with an emphasis in litigation. In addition to this intensive training, I believe that my studies in political science and English have prepared me for a successful career as a paralegal.

I would like to discuss the possibilities of an entry-level position with your firm and appreciate your consideration of my application.

Thank you for your interest, and I look forward to hearing from you soon.

Sincerely yours,

Gordon Shore

320 Roswell Road, North East
Atlanta, Georgia 30062
June 24,1995

Mr. Todd Beauchamp
Adam, Carnes and Warner
1700 Peachtree Road North East
Atlanta, Georgia 30326

Dear Mr. Beauchamp:

In response your ad in the *Atlanta Constitution* of June 23, I would like to apply for the paralegal position listed by your firm.

Recently, I graduated with the degree of Bachelor of Science in Paralegal Studies from Samford University in Birmingham, Alabama. In addition to the intensive paralegal courses, I received computer training and developed strong research skills.

My experience as a legal secretary over the last three years has also given me the opportunity to become familiar with legal procedures. Combined with my undergraduate studies, this experience and training should contribute to my effectiveness as a future paralegal.

I would like to discuss employment opportunities at Adams, Carnes and Warner and demonstrate how my skills and qualifications can meet your needs.

Thank you for your interest and consideration. I will call your office within the next week to set up an appointment at some time convenient to you.

Sincerely yours,

Sheri L. Wilcox

**Sample Cover Letter To Be Included in Mailing
Campaign for Paralegal Position in Banking.**

2801 West Oak Street
Southfield, Michigan 48075
April 21, 1995

Ms. Pamela Thomas
First Reserve Bank of Madison
654 Grace Street
Richmond, Virginia 23219

Dear Ms. Thomas:

As a recent graduate of the American Institute for Paralegal Studies, I am seeking a position that would enable me to utilize my education, skills, and experience.

My background, education, and experience enables me, I strongly believe, to bring a wide range of qualifications to this position. For example, while teaching in the Southfield Public School System, I developed a community program that enabled gifted students to work in local organizations and companies. One such project specifically focused on the banking industry. For three years, I worked closely with all levels of banking personnel to determine ways in which young people could make a contribution to this important aspect of our economy. In doing so, I recognized that my educational background in accounting and additional paralegal training would uniquely qualify me to perform paralegal functions within this setting.

I would welcome the opportunity to meet with you about paralegal positions at First Reserve Bank and discuss how the qualifications I have described could make me an asset to your organization. If convenient, therefore, I would like to set up an appointment to discuss employment possibilities with you. Within the next few days, I will call your office to set up an appointment. Thank you for your interest and consideration.

Sincerely yours,

Steven Goranson

Sample Cover Letter Responding to Blind Ad for Paralegal Position

761 Washington Drive
Arlington Heights, Illinois 60001
June 15, 1995

Box 122, *Chicago Tribune*
Chicago, Illinois 60601

Dear Sir or Madam:

In response to your ad of June 14 in the *Chicago Tribune* listing an entry-level paralegal position, I would like to submit my application.

As a recent graduate of the Institute for Paralegal Studies at Loyola University Chicago, I believe that I bring strong qualifications to an entry-level position. My paralegal training has afforded me the highest level of education, with experienced instructors in the legal field. In addition, the emphasis on computer skills within the program reflects an understanding of the importance of technical expertise for legal assistants. In the generalist curriculum, I also developed skills in legal research, documentation, court briefs, litigation, business law, citing, and shepardizing.

My previous background in English and foreign languages has also added to my proficiency in all areas of written and verbal communication. I am fluent in Spanish as well as English and have used my language skills in business as well as personal settings. These skills, along with my background, training, and experience, could make me an asset to your organization.

I would welcome the opportunity to discuss the paralegal position with you. Please contact me at the above phone number at your earliest convenience. Thank you for your interest and consideration. I look forward to hearing from you.

Sincerely yours,

Maria Mendez

519 West Montrose Place
Sarasota, Florida 32433
March 25, 1995

Mr. Robert Allen
Whitaker, Strom and Bacon
820 Lakeview Boulevard
Orlando, Florida 32816

Dear Mr. Allen:

In response to your ad for a paralegal position in the *Orlando Daily Times* of March 23, I would like to submit my application.

Recently, I completed my certificate program in paralegal studies at Sarasota County Vocational Institute, with an emphasis in corporate law. This program enabled me to improve skills that I have developed in a home-based business I established several years ago. I not only worked with attorneys in setting up proper legal procedures but became aware of all aspects of tax law and filing for small business owners. In addition, I developed and utilized my communication skills, including interpersonal written, verbal, and computer skills. During that time, my interest in the legal field was also sparked, leading me to attain the essential skills I needed to follow a paralegal profession.

My extensive experience in working with the public has required me to be organized, disciplined, energetic, and self-reliant. I strongly believe, therefore, that my personal as well as professional qualifications uniquely qualify me for the position listed. I would welcome an opportunity to demonstrate how I can bring my organizational and problem-solving skills to your firm. I look forward to hearing from you.

Sincerely yours,

Martha Marshall

Sample Cover Letter for Corporate Paralegal Position Listed in Blind Ad

22 North Wilton Drive
Richmond, Virginia 23232
September 12, 1995

Box 808B
Richmond News
Richmond, Virginia 23232

Dear Personnel Manager:

I am applying for the corporate paralegal position listed in the *Richmond News* of September 11, 1995. My background and experience in a legal setting, as well as in the business world, seem particularly appropriate, and I believe that my qualifications could serve the needs of your organization.

With an undergraduate degree in business, I have held various positions as a legal secretary during my undergraduate days and, upon graduation, in the accounting, finance, and business training offices of a major corporation in Virginia. During that time, I developed essential skills that enabled me to perform well within that environment. I came to understand the corporate culture and had the opportunity to use my accounting and business skills in various departments. As I moved into business training, I also developed strong interpersonal, written, and verbal skills.

My additional paralegal training on the corporate track has not only enhanced my interest in the legal field but has demonstrated to me how I can combine these interests with my education, background, and training.

I would welcome an opportunity to discuss how I can bring my skills and qualifications to your firm as an effective paralegal. Thank you for your interest and consideration. I look forward to hearing from you.

Sincerely yours,

Nancy Baldridge

Sample Cover Letter for Career-Changer Applying for Paralegal Position

1220 Saxton Road
Fairview, New Jersey 07022
June 25, 1995

Mr. John Wilkerson
Appleton, Addison and Abrams
2300 Wharton Place
Morristown, New Jersey 07960

Dear Mr. Wilkerson:

In a recent issue of the ***Morristown Community News,*** I read of your firm's renewed dedication to environmental issues. As someone with a strong commitment to the environment and recent completion of a paralegal program that enabled me to develop training and background in this area, I would welcome the opportunity to discuss employment possibilities with your organization.

For years, I worked in community-based organizations as an advocate, public relations coordinator, and newspaper editor. During that time, I came to recognize the importance of public involvement in environmental issues but also realized the importance of gaining skills in this area, so that I could help to effect change in a very direct way. My paralegal training has provided such skills.

Combined with my organizational and communication skills, I now believe that I can bring a strong set of qualifications as a paralegal to an organization such as yours. Within the next week, I will call your office to set up an interview to discuss such a possibility, if that is convenient for you.

Thank you for your interest and consideration. I look forward to meeting you.

Sincerely yours,

David Erickson

Sample Cover Letter for Career-Changer
Applying for Generalist Paralegal Position

567 Martinez Drive
Houston, Texas 77045
May 15, 1995

Mr. Ralph Strauss
Strauss, Held and Holcomb
1220 Southwest Boulevard
Houston, Texas 77049

Dear Mr. Strauss:

The paralegal position listed with your firm in the *Southwest Daily Herald* (May 15,1995) is one for which I believe I am well qualified. Please accept this letter as my application.

Over the last several years, I have developed a wide range of skills in varied settings that have enhanced the recent paralegal training I have completed and the Associate of Applied Science Degree I received at San Jacinto College. These include administrative, management, and strong written and verbal communication skills. Within a research office setting, I was frequently called upon to work under deadline with several supervisors.

With my paralegal education and training, I would now like to utilize these skills in a challenging legal environment. The position described at Strauss, Held and Holcomb appears to be such a position, and I would welcome the opportunity to meet with you to discuss this possibility.

I submit my resumé for your consideration, and I look forward to hearing from you.

Sincerely yours,

Lily Adamcek

Sample Cover Letter for Paralegal Position Listed in Law Journal

9705 Sotweed Drive
Bakersfield, California 93311
June 1, 1995

Mr. Kenneth Delaney
Kenneth Delaney Law Associates
2209 Balboa Boulevard
Bakersfield, California 93319

Dear Mr. Delaney:

I am writing in response to the paralegal position listed in the June issue of the *California Law Journal.* I believe I am strongly qualified and would like to apply.

As a recent graduate of DeAnza College with an Associate of Arts degree and an ABA-approved paralegal certificate, I have developed skills and training that will enable me to meet the challenges of the position you describe. I have extensive background in legal and factual research, and hands-on class experience in drafting interrogatories and preparing deposition questions. In addition, I bring personal qualifications of diligence, reliability, and commitment.

I look forward to meeting you and further discussing this position in an interview. At that time, I will be happy to bring writing samples, personal recommendations, and references.

In the next week, I will call your office to set up an appointment at your convenience. Thank you for your consideration.

Sincerely yours,

Walter Hensley

Sample Cover Letter with Referral

1232 Liverpool Street
Spokane, Washington 99209
August 15, 1995

Ms. Sarah Fulton
Estates and Wills Division
Northwest Savings and Trust Bank
Spokane, Washington 99201

Dear Ms. Fulton:

Annette Carmichael, of the Accounting Department of Northwest Savings and Trust Bank, has informed me of a paralegal position opening with your bank. She believes I am qualified to fill the position and has suggested that I apply.

As a graduate of Spokane Community College, I received an Associate of Arts Degree in Paralegal Studies. During that time, I developed a broad-based knowledge in all aspects of law, including estates, wills, and banking regulations. In addition, I was required to develop legal research skills, and analyze business law agreements. I also completed computer training that could prove to be an asset in this position.

I am eager to begin my paralegal career within a stimulating environment that would enable me to utilize my skills and further develop my interest in the banking industry.

Within the next few days, I will call your office to set up a time to discuss this possibility, if that is convenient for you.

Thank you for your consideration, and I look forward to meeting you.

Sincerely yours,

Adrienne Dupris

Sample Cover Letter in Mass Mailing Campaign for Generalist Paralegal Position

238 Washington Avenue
Omaha, Nebraska 68120
May 15, 1995

Mr. Herbert Sullivan
Sullivan, Weiss and Thatcher
820 Jackson Boulevard
Lincoln, Nebraska 68504

Dear Mr. Sullivan:

As a recent graduate of The College of St. Mary with a Bachelor of Arts in Paralegal Studies, I am currently seeking a challenging paralegal position that will enable me to use my education and training in the legal field.

In addition to the proficiency all students in this program are required to attain in handling a wide range of paralegal responsibilities and duties, I took additional courses in computer training and written communication to enhance those skills that would make me an asset to any organization for which I would be working.

I believe I bring a strong set of personal qualifications to a position, including commitment, enthusiasm, flexibility, and reliability. On campus as well as in my varied work experiences, I have developed a reputation for being well organized, disciplined and hard working. I am eager to bring these personal and professional attributes to a stimulating work setting such as yours, and I would welcome the opportunity to discuss employment possibilities with your firm.

I will call your office within the next week to set up an appointment at a time convenient for you. Thank you for your consideration, and I look forward to meeting you.

Sincerely yours,

Elena Ranalli

6

How to Get Hired: The Art of Being Interviewed

The word *interview* stems from the French word *entre-voir*, which means to "see each other." If we take that meaning one step further, we see in a current English dictionary that the word *interview* literally means "to see each other *mutually*." In other words, the scope and purpose of the interview is to find out if the job candidate and potential employer are "right" for each other. On both sides, it's a risk. So, basically, the interviewing process enables both parties to find out about each other, to "see" each other. It's important to understand this basic point because it emphasizes how and why an applicant should prepare thoroughly for this final step of the job search.

Of all the job search stages, the interview is the single most important step: its goal is the final selling job you must do. And you must learn to do it well. Part of the problem, however, is that many people feel that they have no idea of what they will be asked, and they don't feel that they can do any preparation.

This chapter not only dispels that myth; it shows you the steps to take in preparation for a successful interview.

First of all, it is important to recognize that the interview is an anxiety-producing, stress-filled situation. Of course it is. You have put in long hours, hard work, and a great deal of money preparing for the big job interview. And who likes to be rejected?

You must also remember that the interview is often an irrational, subjective process. A partial reason for this is that people don't realize that although they may seem competent and qualified on paper (the resumé and the cover letter), in person they may come across in quite a different way. After all, it's the *person* who gets hired. And that is what this chapter is all about: showing you how to present yourself, or "sell" yourself, if you will, as the best person for the job.

That leads us to the basic negotiation going on in the interview. The question is, from the interviewer, "Why should I hire *you*?" And the answer from the interviewee must be, "Because I am the best person for the job."

If you keep this basic question in mind, then all of your answers to questions during the interview will be geared to support your contention that you *are* the best person for the job.

Keeping that basic point in mind, let's now examine the steps you can take in developing successful interviewing strategies.

Let's reiterate what we've already said because it bears repeating. For most people, a great part of the fear of being interviewed comes from the fear of the unknown—what is going to happen. And the key to success in interviewing for jobs is the same key you have used for every previous part of your job campaign: preparation.

You may think that an interview may last only thirty minutes to an hour, and so much preparation time could not possibly be warranted. After all, don't they know everything about you? Not quite. They do not know you. Those interview minutes, from their perspective, are crucial. For this reason, these minutes will be the most important time in your job campaign.

Your interview preparation, therefore, should consist of what you need to find out about the organization, the job for which you are applying, and, if possible, the person who will be interviewing you.

Interview Preparation

Information on the Organization

Gain as much information as you can on the company or firm. Who are the key executives? How large is the organization? How many employees are there? What is the volume of sales?

Is it a product or a service organization? What is the specialty or specialties? Does the firm hire paralegals? If so, how many? And how long have they been there?

The more you know about your company, the better prepared you will be to see how *you* fit in. You will also save valuable time during the interview. If you have taken the time and effort to do your homework, you will impress your interviewer as being someone who is truly interested in the job. If you are skillful, you can work this knowledge into a conversation in a very casual way, with appropriate timing. For example, if you are talking about your background or interests, you can make a transition to a comment such as, "I was particularly interested in the position your firm took on the West Chicago case that I read about in *The Law Review.*" Making such references or transitions from a topic to your own interests or background shows that you have well-developed listening skills, so that you are ready to make connections.

Later in this chapter, we will discuss the importance of listening skills and how to develop them. All this is part of the preparation you must do. And for those who complain that they have no time for such preparation, just think of the return you will get on your investment! The impression you make will enable you to stand out from your competition.

But where will you find this information? There are a number of resources available:

- Annual reports
- Articles in business and professional journals
- Bar Association magazines and newsletters
- Dunn and Bradstreet directories
- *Lexis/Nexis* or WESTLAW
- Moody's directories
- Newspapers (including regional trade papers and local newspapers) and magazines
- Placement agencies, if they have arranged the interview
- Standard and Poor's directories

Finally, remember your personal contacts. Do you know anyone who works for the organization or knows someone who does? Professional associations are also a good source of information on companies.

Information on the Job for Which You are Applying

Find out as much as you can about paralegal positions within the organization, using the same resources mentioned above. In addition, the more you can discuss your role as a paralegal and how you can be an asset to the company, the more you will impress your interviewer.

It is also acceptable for *you* to have questions about the job and the role of the paralegal within the organization. Would it be possible for you to meet and talk to other paralegals who work there? Intelligent and thoughtful questions will demonstrate your professional interest in the field, as well as the position.

Information on the Interviewer

Find out the exact name of the interviewer, if at all possible, either over the phone when the interview is scheduled or from the receptionist when you come in to the interview. Make certain that you have the correct name and pronunciation. There are instances in which interviewers who have been otherwise impressed by a candidate have ruled out that person because he or she made an error in pronouncing the interviewer's name.

Any other relevant information about the interviewer may prove very useful to you, if it is available, such as what the interviewer does within the company, or the interviewer's background. Is the interviewer the person for whom you would be working? Will the interviewer be the person making the final decision concerning the job? The purpose of such information is not to enable you to offer contrived statements but rather, to illustrate that you are sufficiently interested in the position to find out as much as you can about the company and its staff. Listen carefully to what the interviewer is saying so that you can make connections to your own qualifications for the job. Doing so will confirm in the interviewer's mind that you are person with similar goals and interests who would be compatible, if you do share these interests. In other words, you are getting the interviewer to see you as a person and to like you.

Two final suggestions: Students should not hesitate to ask their teachers or members of the paralegal training staff if they know anything about a firm. Also, when you are called for an interview with a firm that you have not heard of, ask a few questions: What kind of law does this firm practice? How large is it? You needn't spend an extraordinary amount of time over the phone asking these questions before the interview, but a few basic questions will reveal your interest in the firm *and* will also give you some idea of the kind of work paralegals do on the job.

Preparing Yourself for the Interview

In preparing yourself for the interview, try to put yourself in the place of the person who will be interviewing you. He or she is interested in finding an employee who can make a contribution to the company, get along with other employees, and promote the image that the company wants to project. In other words, your *professional appearance* and *behavior* may single you out and rate you higher than other applicants whose credentials may be as good as yours or even better.

Remember that your qualifications have already been submitted and have been recognized as appropriate for the position, along with those of other applicants. The purpose of the interview is for a potential employer to assess you: to measure your professional attitude about your work, to evaluate your experience and accomplishments as they relate to this particular job, and to determine how effectively you handle yourself in a stressful situation—your interpersonal and verbal communication skills. If these were not essential characteristics to an employer, the resumé itself would have gotten you the job!

How to Make a Good First Impression

According to a recent survey, employers are looking for a person with strong organizational skills, competence, reliability, flexibility, and the ability to become part of the team. They want to know how you will will fit in.

The fact of the matter is that personal chemistry often sells a candidate. You would do well to focus on some of the following intangible areas in order to make that important first impression as positive as possible.

It is impossible for you to change your personality radically, nor would you want to. You might consider, however, ways in which you can tailor your image to suit a company's needs. If you feel that your individuality is being threatened by conforming to a company's dress code, for example, remember that the choice is yours in whether or not to apply for a position within a particular company. Generally speaking, certain traits are desirable in a job applicant. They are part of the packaging that will enable the interviewer to size you up in the first minute or two—the time in which it takes us to form our first impressions. These impressions which, incidentally, are very hard to overcome. Think of your own personal experiences with negative impressions you have formed of certain people, impressions that later proved to be erroneous. This important first impression, therefore, influences all the subsequent impressions—and frequently determines whether or not you are offered the job. What goes into creating this favorable first impression, and how can you work on creating the impression you want to convey?

First of all, let's eliminate the notion that this discussion is about superficialities or mere externals. That is often the argument for those who disagree with the "first impression" theory. We are talking about presenting a professional package that gives an interviewer an immediate idea of who you are, based on what he or she sees. The interview itself will either support or invalidate this first impression, but why take the chance of having an impression work against you?

Wardrobe and Grooming

The first clue to your professionalism is your personal grooming. An interviewer will try to see you in the job. What should you wear? When in doubt, err on the side of being conservative. High-quality clothes rather than trendy outfits are a good investment. You are entering a conservative profession that respects understatement in dress. As a guideline, dress in the style you expect to wear when meeting a client or accompanying an attorney to court.

A suit is recommended garb for women and men. Dark colors are appropriate. For women, neutral colors such as beige, taupe or navy are suggested. This is true for coordinates such as blouses, as well. Colors may be fine as accents, but avoid large flowers or prints that may be distracting. Women should also pay attention to the materials they choose. While cotton and linen may be appropriate on the job, they will become wrinkled after a very short time. On the other hand, polyester does not offer a professional look.

These may seem like such inconsequential details, but they are all related to the impression you give as you walk through the door for that interview. Let your wardrobe be your first introduction before you even open your mouth. If you are still hesitant about what to wear, talk to a friend whose professional taste in clothes you admire. Or you might consult with someone in the professional or career women's section in a local department store. These consultants have become very popular and can be very helpful. One young woman who was apprehensive about what to wear to an interview stood outside an office and waited until the employees came out for lunch, so she could see what *they* were wearing!

Whatever you decide, remember that your clothes should not distract from you in any way. Also remember that good grooming entails more than clothes. Women should avoid heavy makeup, perfume, sunglasses, dangling jewelry, bulky handbags, and hats (that you don't remove). For men, shirts without jackets or ties, and unshined shoes all can build up a negative impression. Do not chew gum during an interview.

Personal Attributes

Below is a discussion of the major personal and professional traits that interviewers have identified as positive qualities. Effective listening skills and appropriate body language are important and are therefore the main topics of the discussion. Other important traits are also listed.

Effective Listening Skills

1. Make eye contact with the interviewer, but do not stare. Pay attention to what is being said.

2. Avoid interrupting, even if what you have to say is directly related to a comment being made. Do not dominate the conversation in an effort to impress the interviewer with your knowledge.

3. Do not jump in immediately with your comments, particularly if the interviewer is not yet finished speaking. Do not override the interviewer's comments.

4. Answer the question being asked. If you do not know the answer, don't try to impress the interviewer by bluffing. On the other hand, do not answer a question that has not been asked. If you are not certain about the best way to answer a question, rather than give a rambling answer, ask that the question be qualified. For example, if the interviewer says "Tell me something about yourself," respond with "Would you like to hear something about my personal background or work history?"

5. Avoid making confrontational remarks if you do not agree with a statement made by the interviewer.

6. Do not try to fill up short silences with needless talking. On the other hand, learn to use silence as a transition to saying something you would like the interviewer to know about you.

7. If you are not certain what the question was, rephrase what you think you have heard, to make certain that your perception is accurate. This is an important skill to develop, particularly if you feel that a comment or question has put you on the defensive.

Positive Body Language

Without opening your mouth, you convey messages and attitudes by how you sit, stand, use your hands. Be sure the message is a positive one and works for you. Here are some tips for doing this:

1. Remain standing as long as the interviewer is standing.

2. When you sit down, avoid slouching.

3. Do not put your arms on the interviewer's desk. On the other hand, leaning slightly forward in your chair indicates interest.

4. Avoid crossing your arms or assuming any confrontational poses. Crossed arms, fidgeting, and crossed legs create a "closed" appearance, despite your positive verbal communication.

5. Do not gesture during the conversation or make emphatic hand movements.

6. Do not cover your mouth when you speak.

7. Avoid gazing off when you answer a question. While you may think this reflects serious thought, it can seem very artificial or even condescending. And although you should not stare, it is appropriate for you to make frequent eye contact with your interviewer.

8. Men should keep their hands out of their pockets when speaking.

9. Women should avoid twisting their hair or making any other distracting movements.

Other Important Personal Traits

Here are some other positive traits that interviewers have identified:

- Verbal communication with: good diction, proper grammar, and no slang
- Enthusiasm and energy
- Flexibility and adaptability
- Imagination, creativity, and resourcefulness
- Positive attitude
- Honesty
- Sincerity
- Persuasiveness
- Poise
- Logical and well-organized thinking

As you review this list, you will notice that a person's professional competence is not included. What that indicates is that it is a given that you are a good worker and that you are qualified. Your resumé should attest to this, and you should be able to convince the interviewer of it. The traits listed above are those personal and professional characteristics that will determine whether you fit in, whether you are the right person for the job, and therefore, whether you should be offered the job. These are traits that all employers value highly. Some of them you will develop with experience; if you identify any of these areas as your own personal weaknesses, you can take steps to turn them into positive qualities. But you must begin with an honest self-evaluation and then move into directions you can take to improve yourself. Once you develop these qualities your level of self-confidence will soar—and employers can spot *that* quality immediately.

One interviewer summed it up by saying that he looks for "presence" in a job candidate, an indication that the applicant understands what the job entails and is confident that he or she is the best person to do it.

You might say that during an interview lasting one-half to an hour, no one could possibly detect all of the above qualities and others as well. But you would be surprised at how many of these qualities quickly come to the surface in a brief interchange of ideas. And remember that an interviewer is looking for those *particular* qualities. How you look and what you say may not be the only index to your personality and your qualifications, but this is the only opportunity your interviewer has to find out about you.

The intangible qualities of sincerity, poise, alertness, and thoughtfulness cannot easily be analyzed. It is usually a combination of elements such as posture, reaction, and attitude in general that creates a personal dynamic or chemistry that will sell you as an applicant.

No one wants to hire a negative, pessimistic person, no matter how impressive his or her credentials. On the other hand, you harm yourself if you try to develop an unnatural or flamboyant personality. What you must do is recognize your own style, try to eliminate your personal weaknesses, and develop your unique strengths. It all comes down to learning how to be confident in yourself and developing the skills to convey this confidence.

Here are some tips for a successful interview:

1. Develop a good, firm handshake.

2. Avoid stammering. It is far better to indicate that you would like to think about the answer to a question if you do not know it.

3. Observe your interviewer's interests and background. You may want to use some of this information in your follow-up letter.

4. Listen. Try to find out what happened to the last person in this position; this can be an indication of how rapid the turnover is, unless it is a new position. Find out about the company's method of handling finances, budgetary policies, and any other details that pertain to the job you want.

5. Have questions prepared to fill in gaps of long silence. Later in this chapter is a list of questions you could have on hand. It is perfectly acceptable to come prepared with a small notebook in which you have written your questions or in which you might jot down questions during the interview. Use good judgment, and avoid being conspicuous if you do this.

6. Interest and enthusiasm are important, but no matter how much you may want the job, it is usually unwise to accept any offer, no matter how attractive it looks, on the spur of the moment. An employer will not rescind the offer if you request some time (a few days or a week, at the most) to think about it. That will give you time to come up with any questions you may have.

7. On the other hand, do not hesitate to ask, at the end of the interview, what time limit they have set on making their decision for hiring.

8. Finally, it is a good idea to scout out the location of the interview, including where to park, and travel time, if you are not familiar with the area. Do this before the day of the interview. Doing so will lower your stress level before the actual interview.

Here are some things you will want to take with you when you go to an interview:

1. Take a leather portfolio or briefcase, similar to one you will actually be using on the job. Make certain it is leather, even if you have to borrow it from a friend.

2. Take a professional-quality pen that works. Try it before the interview.

3. Take a notepad for jotting down notes during the interview. You may also have a list of your own questions on this pad.

4. Take extra copies of your resumé that are printed, not photocopied. Five or six copies are sufficient.

5. Take a list of your references, with addresses and telephone numbers. The paper should match your resumé.

6. Take a sheet with all the dates of employment, with specific salaries. You may not need this sheet, but it could be useful in negotiating your salary.

7. Take writing samples, articles you have written or cowritten (or articles that mention you). Sample briefs from your paralegal training courses are also useful.

8. Take money for parking and change for phone calls.

9. Some women have carried extra pantyhose, to avoid embarrassment if they snag or run their hosiery.

While such precautions may seem excessive, remember that the more you prepare for your interview, in ways that you *can* prepare, the less anxiety your will have.

Here are some things to *avoid* in an interview:

1. Do not arrive late. Even if the location is a new one to you, if you plan your route and schedule your time beforehand, you should not have a problem. If the interview is around rush hour and you are driving, you can plan accordingly if you know where you are going. If you are using public transportation, keep in mind that trains and buses are frequently late. That should not be an excuse for you to be late. Give yourself enough time. Plan to be ten to fifteen minutes early. Arriving any earlier can make you appear overly anxious. You can always walk around the block or wait in a building lobby if you are too early.

2. Leave your outerwear in the outer office. There is usually a closet or coat rack for this purpose.

3. Never apologize for your lack of experience or credentials, or anything you may perceive as a liability. Remember that someone thought you were qualified for this position; otherwise, you would not have been called in for an interview.

4. Do not chew gum or eat mints. Do not bring in coffee, juice, or any other type of container.

5. Do not smoke.

6. Avoid negative comments about a past employer, colleague, or organization. Avoid discussions of a personal or potentially volatile nature, such as those regarding race, politics, religion, or feminist issues.

7. Do not lose your temper. If you do not agree with the interviewer's point of view, and even if you are asked an illegal question, remain calm. Remember that you are under no obligation to accept the job or work for this organization. You want to leave the interviewer with the best impression of you by being professional in your demeanor.

8. Do not sermonize or overpower the conversation in an effort to sell yourself. The line between being confident and arrogant is frequently a fine one. If you oversell yourself in an effort to appear confident, you may lose the job. This is where practicing before the interview can be useful. A friend's appraisal of your performance may help you to set the right tone in answering questions, particularly difficult ones.

9. Although you want to project self-confidence, be careful about sounding too cocky. Be realistic about your talents and qualifications, but remember that a touch of modesty helps.

10. Be courteous but not effusive or insincere.

11. Do not call the interviewer by his or her first name, no matter how friendly he or she may appear. On the other hand, avoid using "sir" or "ma'am," because such forms of address make you sound inappropriately subordinate to the interviewer.

12. Do not wear sunglasses. Make eye contact with your interviewer.

13. Do not tap on the desk, jingle change, or display any other nervous mannerisms. If you are unaware of your nervous gestures, ask a friend to alert you to them. Once you are aware of them try to avoid them.

14. Do not look at your watch. Let the interviewer set the pace of the interview. Be alert to the interviewer's actions. When he or she gets up, that is a cue that the interview is over.

15. Do not ask, "Will I get the job?" or "Can I have the job?" Rather, state, "I hope that you will consider me for this position. I really am interested."

16. Do not ask about salary until later on in the hiring process, perhaps at a second interview. The interviewer will generally bring it up. If it is brought up immediately in the first interview, simply postpone the discussion by indicating that you would like to first know more about the position and what it entails.

17. Do not be evasive. If a question seems too personal, indicate how you feel about it but perhaps you misinterpreted what the interviewer was asking. As subtly as possible, change the topic. For example, you could refer to a previous discussion and ask a relevant question.

Now that you have some idea of what employers are looking for, let's examine the actual interview and what goes on.

The Interview

Arriving for the Interview

You should arrive approximately fifteen minutes early. The receptionist may hand you an application form to complete. In some firms, the interviewer may be notified of your arrival immediately. This means that you are being observed, in terms of your efficiency in handling a routine form. Therefore, you will be at an advantage if you simply complete the basic items: name, address, telephone number, social security number, date, and position for which you are applying. In the section entitled work experience or work history, attach a copy of your resumé that you have brought and write, "See Resume." You do not need to complete the section requesting your salary requirements. Print all information legibly with a professional pen that you have already used and know works properly. Do not use pencil.

If you are asked to wait, use the time to observe your surroundings rather than become engrossed in reading materials. You may also want to review another copy of your resumé that you have brought along.

If you are detained for any length of time, it is reasonable for you to ask the receptionist if you understood correctly the time you were scheduled to come, particularly if you have scheduled another interview for the same day. This can be a courteous request; the manner of your question should assure this.

Beginning the Interview

The interviewer ushers you into his or her office, and you both try to establish some rapport. Sometimes this can be as casual as commenting on a recent major event such as the weather, sports or other areas of small talk. Some cautions: Do not use this opening phase as a time to criticize or complain about anything such as faulty directions given you, the difficult commute, heavy traffic, or anything else that would mark you as a complainer. Use caution also in any compliments you may feel obligated to offer. Avoid personal comments on photographs, unless they arise naturally from the conversation (for example, you are discussing a sporting event and the interviewer has a photograph displaying a trophy). Anything personal may be totally inappropriate, so follow the lead of the interviewer in this opening phase.

Questions You May Be Asked During the Interview

Remember that you have already begun the interview, so let the interviewer set the pace and begin the serious questioning. Below is a list of questions you may be asked, so be prepared to answer them. As you review this list, you will notice that some of these questions are broad and general. It is your job to answer them as specifically as you can, relating your answers to the position for which you are being interviewed.

The questions may be asked in any order. Usually, an interviewer will want to get some background information first. That may not be the case in your situation, however. It is also important to recognize that not all interviewers are good interviewers. Some may be prepared, and others may not be. You may have an interviewer who knows the job and is eager to get the very best person. The questions may be incisive or thought provoking. Other interviewers may not be interested or even competent. So it's important for you to assess the situation as soon as you can. Doing so may help you to understand how and why certain questions are being asked and help you to understand the role of the interviewer.

Later on in this chapter, a list of illegal or discriminatory questions is included. If you are asked these questions, try to give a general reply that will reveal your professionalism. If you confront the interviewer with the illegality of the question, the situation may become unpleasant. Remember that you do not need to accept this position; however, it is important for you to be graceful and professional in *your* behavior. If you know how you will handle any illegal questions *before* the interview, your anxiety level will be minimized.

You will also be wise to prepare answers (although that does not mean formula answers) to typical questions that are often asked. Below is a list of such questions.

Questions You May Be Asked During an Interview

- Tell me something about yourself.

- Why did you decide to become a paralegal?

- What made you change fields?

- Why do you think you would like to work for us?

- What is important to you in a job?

- What do you think determines a person's progress in a company?

- How do you feel about traveling on the job?

- What about working overtime and on weekends?

- What are your own special abilities and skills?

- What is your major strength?

- What is your major weakness?

- Can you take instructions and criticism without getting upset?

- Do you prefer to work individually or with others?

- What type of boss do you prefer?

- Have you ever had difficulties getting along with your bosses?

- How do you like routine work?

- Are you a detailed person?

- What motivates you in a job?

- What was the best part of your last job? The worst part?

- Where do you think you'd like to be five years from now?

- Are you interested in going to law school?

- How would you describe yourself, if you were another person talking about you?

- You seem overqualified. Do you think you would be happy in this job?

Questions You May Ask During an Interview

Do not hesitate to ask questions *you* may have about the job. You might prepare a brief list. It will impress the interviewer that you have thought about the job and the company before coming in. While you may want to jot down a question or two during the interview, make certain that you do so discretely. Pulling out a memo pad at the beginning of the interview to take notes will not impress the interviewer.

Below is a list of questions you may ask. Add your own questions to the list, or modify it to fit the situation and the position.

Questions You May Ask During An Interview

- Is this a new position?
- If so, why is this position needed?
- To whom would I report?
- Will I be working for more than one attorney?
- What are the minimum billable hours for paralegals?
- How many hours do the paralegals work, on average?
- Is traveling involved?
- Are paralegals considered part of the support staff or the professional staff?
- Is clerical help available?
- What are the major responsibilities of the job?
- Will I have an opportunity to meet with other paralegals currently working in your firm?
- Is there any kind of paralegal orientation for newcomers?
- What access will I have to a library for LEXIS/NEXIS or WESTLAW?
- Will there be someone to train me in new areas?
- Does your firm encourage continuing education and professional development?
- What major problems would I encounter on this job?
- When do you think you will be making your hiring decision?

List your own special interests, concerns, or questions you may have about the job:

_____

_____

_____

Difficult Questions You May Be Asked During an Interview and How to Handle Them

Federal regulations prohibit an interviewer from asking questions that indicate discrimination in the hiring process. This does not mean that these questions will not crop up in some form. Be prepared, therefore, to answer these questions in a way that will serve you best.

For example, if an interviewer asks you about your family responsibilities and care of your small children, if you have any, make certain that you convey that you have already prepared for their care should any problem arise. The same holds true if you are asked about your marital status or plans for having a family. Make your answer brief, but focus on the importance of your professional commitment at this point.

If questions arise about your willingness or availability to travel or work overtime (if that is a part of the job), again stress how you (and your spouse and family) have thought about this possibility and have agreed that it would be possible for you to handle such situations, providing you have time to make any arrangements that would be necessary.

Any questions about your spouse's profession, salary, interests, or career goals should be answered in a way that divulges the minimum amount of information.

Legally, you are not required to answer any questions that are not directly related to the job and that may demonstrate some form of discrimination, such as questions relating to age, race, politics, or any issues concerning your family or personal life.

The more you can anticipate difficult questions and prepare for them, the more your anxieties will be alleviated before going into the interview.

What would be the most difficult question for *you* to answer? One that you hope will not be asked? Plan on how you would answer such a question. If you are not asked, the issue becomes irrelevant. If you *are* asked, at least you will have considered an appropriate response.

For example, are you concerned about long gaps in your employment history? If so, think about how you have kept yourself abreast of current issues; have developed skills in various volunteer positions; and attended workshops, lectures, and continuing education programs.

Do you feel that age is a factor for you? Think of all the positive characteristics that you can bring to a job such as maturity, reliability, decisiveness, good judgment, an awareness of people, and the ability to handle conflicts. In other words, once you convince yourself you could be an asset to a firm, you can convince an employer with much greater ease.

Responses to Difficult Questions

The previous information summarizes how to prepare yourself for handling difficult questions. Below are some specific ways in which you can protect yourself without alienating the interviewer who poses questions that are illegal or border on illegality.

It can be a touchy, uncomfortable situation, particularly if the job looks attractive. So you may want to ask yourself if this person reflects the attitudes of the organization or is simply uninformed or inexperienced as an interviewer. At any rate, if you are confronted with such questions, try to respond in a way that will work to your advantage.

Below are some typical questions and answers that may offer you some clues on how to handle such questions if they are posed in your interview. One technique is to rephrase the question. Another is to provide as brief an answer as possible and then make a transition to another topic that is directly job related.

1. *Family issues:*

Q. Do you plan to have a family? (Men are usually not asked this question.)

A. At this stage in my career, I am committed to spending my time and energy to a full-time job.

Q. What will you do if your family becomes ill? (If it has been established that you already have a family.)

A. Although my children (son or daughter) have a history of good health and regular checkups, if they require medical attention, I have made arrangements with (spouse, friend, neighbor, relative) to be on call. In an emergency, of course, I would have to make contingent plans, but I have established a reliable support system.

2. *Working overtime:*

Q. How does your spouse feel about you working overtime?

A. We've discussed these possibilities and have agreed that our schedules are flexible enough to handle what the job requires. Of course, it's always easier to have advance notice, whenever possible, to make any necessary arrangements or reschedule something.

3. *Availability for travel:*

Q. Would you be available for traveling?

A. Depending upon the amount of time involved, I don't have any problem with traveling, if I can plan ahead. (Remember, you must decide if you want to travel. This is a good time for you to ask how much travel will be involved and then make your decision accordingly.)

4. *Age issues*

(Note: The age issue may come up in many forms. The basic question being asked here is, "Are you too old to handle this job?")

Q. How do you feel about working for younger people?

A. (Depending upon the context of the question): I've been around young people for most of my life, particularly my own children, and I've not only learned from them, but I've developed respect for them. I know I can bring that ability to this job, whatever the age of my supervisor or boss. Age is never a barrier, as far as I'm concerned. It's the person's attitude toward age and how well he or she gets along with people that's important.

These are just some examples of how to approach difficult questions. Now list the toughest questions you think you might be asked, and prepare the answers. In doing so, you will be readying yourself for a successful interview.

5. *I hope they never ask: Questions that would be difficult for me to answer in an interview, with answers I could give:*

_____

_____

_____

_____

_____

_____

_____

Discriminating Questions

Federal Laws and Regulations Concerning Discrimination in Employment

1. Executive Order 11246, amended by 11375, prohibits discrimination in employment practices (hiring, promotions, benefits, training, salaries) on the basis of race, color, religion, national origin, or sex for all the employers with federal contracts over ten thousand dollars. Report violations to Office of Federal Contract Compliance of the Department of Labor, Washington, D.C. 20210.

2. Age Discrimination in Employment Act prohibits discrimination in employment practices (hiring, salaries, discharge). Report violations to the

Wage and Hour Division of the Employment Standards Administration of the Department of Labor, Washington, D.C. 20210.

3. Title VII of the Civil Rights Act prohibits discrimination in employment practices on the basis of race, color, national origin, sex, or religion for all employers with fifteen or more employees. Report violations to Equal Employment Opportunity Commission, 1800 G Street NE, Washington, D.C. 20506.

4. Equal Pay Act prohibits discrimination in salaries, including most fringe benefits, on the basis of sex. Report violations to Wage and Hour Division of the Employment Standards Administration, Department of Labor, Washington, D.C. 20210.

Discriminatory Questions That May Not Be Asked on Application Forms or During an Interview

1. Questions cannot be asked concerning the applicant's race, religious affiliation, birthplace, or the birthplace of the applicant's parents.

2. An applicant cannot be required to submit a birth certificate, naturalization certificate or baptismal record. (Note: It is no longer discriminatory to require such records once an applicant is hired, since recent federal immigration laws require employers to document United States citizenship for employment eligibility.)

3. An applicant cannot be required to submit a personal photograph with a job application. After a person is hired, a photograph may be required for identification purposes.

4. Questions cannot be asked concerning an applicant's date of birth or age unless such information is needed to ascertain that the applicant meets minimum age requirements.

5. Questions cannot be asked concerning an applicant's native language or the language the applicant commonly uses at home.

6. Inquiries cannot be made about an applicant's military experience in forces other than the United States Armed Forces.

7. Inquiries cannot be made about an applicant's draft status, although it is legal to ask whether an applicant has received any notice to report for duty in the Armed Forces.

8. Questions cannot be asked about an applicant's memberships in any organizations other than professional, trade, or service organizations.

9. Questions cannot be asked about an applicant's arrest record (although a conviction record may be requested.)

10. Inquiries cannot be made about an applicant's relatives, except for who should be notified in emergencies.

11. Inquiries cannot be made about an applicant's marital status, number of children, or plans for having a family.

Salary Negotiations

The question of salary is undoubtedly one of the most delicate points that you have to negotiate, but inevitably it will come up, and you must be prepared to bargain for what you feel you are worth and you can get. If at all possible, the discussion of salary and other employee benefits should be delayed until a job offer has been made, or at least until it has been made clear to you that you are being considered very seriously for the position. Obviously, this can happen only after the interviewer has had an opportunity to talk with you or even call you in for a second interview.

If the question comes up early in the interview (such as, "What is the minimum salary you will accept?"), your best strategy is to use some kind of delaying tactic. For example, you could reply, "That's difficult to answer right now. It would depend on the job and its responsibilities, and I'd like to know more before I can answer."

The purpose of postponing salary discussion is so that you can impress the interviewer with your presentation of yourself. Eventually, however, if both of you establish a mutual interest, you will have to confront the salary issue. And the more you know about salary ranges for paralegals in the area, the better prepared you are to discuss this topic.

Before the interview is the time to do your salary investigation, not during the interview. You cannot negotiate until you have some idea of what the general range is in the field. You must also know your own minimum requirements. Otherwise, you waste your time if the company cannot pay you what you need to earn. Salary scales are not usually available, but you can find information on salary ranges from a paralegal association in the area in which you want to work.

If there is a range within a company, bargain for the top of the range; the company will want you, of course, to agree on the lower part of the range. With persuasion on your part of what you have to offer the organization, the idea is for you to agree on what is mutually acceptable. If the salary is fixed, however (and ask if the salary offered you is a firm one), then ask what other benefits are available and when you can have a salary review. Doing so demonstrates your ambition as well as your initiative. Finally, only you can decide on what salary is fair and what is acceptable to you. Again, doing your homework is essential before you can make a decision.

Closing the Interview and Planning Your Follow-up Strategy

You will probably have some clues as to when the interview is over. The interviewer will either stand or ask if you have any questions about the job.

That is your chance to ask questions you did not have an opportunity to ask earlier, but even more important, it is the time for you to appraise how well you did, if you are interested in the job.

The interviewer may offer definite feedback by the type of comments or questions he or she asks. That may take the form of planning the next step. If that does not happen, try to get some indication of your possible chances for the job. You can do this easily without appearing brash. For example, if you have no clue from the interviewer, you may simply ask, "Is there anything more about my background or experience you would like to know, as it relates to this job?" Or, "Do I seem to have the kind of experience that you're looking for?" These kinds of questions can elicit favorable comments, negative ones, or noncommittal ones. If there is not a definite interest exhibited at this point, you can support your case in the follow-up letter.

Whatever the outcome of the interview, your follow-up letter marks you as a professional who is also courteous. Try to remember the interests and needs of the employer and refer to them in the letter, stressing again how you feel qualified for the job and would enjoy working for the organization now that you have had an opportunity to find out more about it. Keep the letter brief, but be sure to end it on the note that you look forward to hearing from the interviewer concerning the position. Sample letters are included in the next chapter. Be certain to tailor the specific details to your own situation.

You will hear, one way or the other. If the interviewer is interested, you may be called in for a second interview, particularly if salary negotiations were not finalized. A phone call from the company is always a good sign, although it may not necessarily mean that the job is definite. It may be a call for a second interview. Regrets and rejections always come in the form of a letter, sometimes weeks after the job is filled.

If you are interested in the job, however, and send your follow-up letter after the interview, it is perfectly acceptable to call the company within a week or so to see if they made their decision or when they expect to make it. If you are turned down, you may politely ask why. Sometimes you will get a direct, specific answer that will help you later on. You may also get a general response that stresses the number of qualified candidates who had applied for the position. All you can do at this point is review the steps you have taken and analyze your interview.

To help you evaluate your interview performance, keep a log and record your reactions as soon after the interview as possible. The following model provides a format for this recordkeeping and self-evaluation. Recognizing what you did right and what you could have done better will help you to improve your interviewing skills.

Most of us have had the experience of wishing we had said something or not said something during an interview. Such regrets may hamper our chance for success at subsequent interviews. In order to avoid this trap, try to make an honest self-evaluation and learn from each of your interviewing experiences. Practicing with another person may also help you; ask your teachers or members of your local paralegal association whether they would be willing to do a mock interview with you.

A Note on Informational Interviews

Informational interviews are exactly what the title implies. They are not interviews for a specific job opening, but are valuable opportunities for you to learn specific information about a firm or organization, such as how the firm operates, the role of paralegals, the employer's view of the job market, the employer's advice regarding your specific background and experience, and types of paralegal positions for which you would be best suited. The goal of this type of interview is for you to develop interviewing skills, without the stress or anxiety that accompanies an actual job interview. But just as important, the interview enables you find out what a certain job is really like.

If you impress someone at an informational interview, that person will very likely keep you in mind if a job opening occurs. For that reason, you should follow the same process in sending a follow-up thank you letter and enclosing a current resumé for that company's future reference. It is also important for you to keep a log of these interviews.

Review the resources and reference materials in this book to help you identify the most appropriate information sources, including directories, guides, and association encyclopedias. Do not overlook your networking contacts in setting up your informational interviews. A detailed discussion of networking is discussed in a later chapter.

Information Interview Log

Name of Firm	Interviewer's Name and Title	Interview Date	Follow-up Date	Comments

Job Interview Log

Name of Firm Address, Phone	Interviewer's Name and Title	Interview Date	Follow-up Date	Comments

Interview Log Self-Evaluation Chart

Interview Date	Name of Firm	Positive Points	Negative Points

Some points you may wish to include are given below. Add your own points to the list.

Positive Points:

Good chemistry with interviewer

Congenial atmosphere

Answered questions confidently and directly

Interviewer seemed to focus on my strengths

Job described clearly

Other: _____

_____

Negative Points:

Interviewer not interested

Forgot to bring up important information

Felt uncomfortable and nervous

Felt rushed in answering

Did not feel comfortable about appearance

Was late for appointment

Did not understand questions asked

Lacked confidence

Other: _____

_____

The purpose of this self-evaluation is so that you can recognize your weaknesses and overcome them as you continue the interviewing process. Make extra sheets for each interview.

Following Up on the Interview

It is very important for you to write a brief follow-up letter a day or so after your interview, whatever your self-evaluation. These letters should never be handwritten, inasmuch as they will be placed in your file. The next chapter offers you sample letters. Remember that this will be another opportunity for you to highlight what you can bring to the company; it will provide a chance for you to include anything you may have forgotten to mention during the interview itself; and it will also be an appropriate place for you to address any concerns the interviewer may have had about your qualifications for the job.

Review your self-evaluation chart to help you write this letter.

7

Follow-Up Letters

A day or so after the interview has taken place, it is very important for you to write a follow-up letter to the person or persons who interviewed you. In doing so, you not only impress the interviewer with your courtesy, but you remind him or her of how much you are really interested in the position and how well qualified you are to fill it. The letter should be brief and reiterate what you believe are your strengths, as well as your suitability for the position. Some of the following letters illustrate how you can easily focus on these points.

Again, write individual letters and customize your correspondence to the specific interviewer and job.

Follow-up letters take time and care, but if you are willing to put forth the effort, you may well be ahead of the majority of those interviewed who do not send such a letter.

The samples included here are brief, to the point, and cover the variety of responses you might want to send.

Below are some guidelines for your follow-up letter:

1. Thank the interviewer for his or her their interest and valuable time spent in considering you for the position.

2. If possible, refer to some part of the personal conversation, such as shared interests or organizational goals.

3. Express your enthusiasm for the position.

4. Reinforce your strengths and the reasons why you think you are particularly suited for the position.

5. If the interviewer had any concerns about your liabilities or lack of qualifications or experience, be certain to address how you can compensate for any weaknesses by the strengths you bring to the position. For example, you can stress how your skills and experience in your past jobs could make you an asset to the firm or how your maturity could be a contribution to such a fast-paced environment.

6. Refer to the next step in the process: "I look forward to hearing from you soon about your decision."

If you get the job, send an acceptance letter to confirm the starting date and time. Even if you do not get the job, a follow-up letter demonstrates a truly professional attitude.

Follow-up Letter After First Interview

2802 Orchard Avenue
Chicago, Illinois 60604
May 28, 1995

Mr. Wayne Smith
Community Bank
International Department
1822 West Madison Street
Chicago, Illinois 60607

Dear Mr. Smith:

It was a pleasure meeting you today to discuss the job opening in the International Department of Community Bank.

The position is an opportunity for me to use my background, training, and language skills in a stimulating environment. In reviewing your plans for the department's expansion, I am even more enthusiastic about the contributions I could make as a paralegal.

Again, thank you for your interest and consideration. I hope that we will be working together in the future.

If you have any additional questions, please do not hesitate to call me at (312) 935-2120.

Sincerely yours,

Mark Harrison

Follow-up Letter After First Interview

2893 South Hamlin
Des Plaines, Illinois 60016
August 2, 1995

Mr. John Downey
Wentworth, Katz and Walter Associates
One North Dearborn Street
Chicago, Illinois 60602

Dear Mr. Downey:

Thank you for the opportunity to discuss the paralegal opening at Wentworth, Katz and Walter Associates. I enjoyed discussing the company's present commitment and future plans. It is a lively and challenging work environment, and I know that I could bring valuable business experience and skills to the position.

I hope that we will be working together in the future, and I look forward to hearing from you sometime soon. If you have questions or need more information, please call me at (708) 828-3292.

Sincerely,

Felicia Simmons

Follow-up Letter From Applicant out of Job Market for Several Years

761 Summit Drive
Atlanta, Georgia 30328
June 1, 1995

Ms. Katherine Lewis
Saller, DuPont and Flint
2210 Parkway West
Atlanta, Georgia 30319

Dear Ms. Lewis:

Thank you for your time and interest in considering me for a paralegal position at Saller, DuPont and Flint. It was such an enjoyable experience meeting with you and other paralegal staff members, I know that I would thrive in such a creative environment. Your department is lively, energetic, and productive.

I believe my background, skills, experiences, and maturity would enable me to bring a new perspective to your organization. I hope that you agree.

Please call me if I can provide further information or if you have additional questions. I can be reached at (616) 430-1828.

I look forward to hearing from you soon.

Sincerely yours,

Margaret Thornton

Job Acceptance Letter

1021 Wynwood Drive
Grand Rapids, Michigan 49501
August 18,1995

Mr. Harold Henderson
Henderson Law Associates
212 West Wesley Street
Grand Rapids, Michigan 49012

Dear Mr. Henderson:

I am pleased to accept the paralegal position at Henderson Law Associates.

September 15, the day you suggested, is fine as a starting date, and I will report to you and Mr. Simpson at 9:00 a.m. in the first floor conference room.

In the meantime, thank you for this opportunity to begin my paralegal career with such a prestigious firm. I look forward to making a contribution to Henderson Law Associates.

Sincerely yours,

Marcia Morgan

Follow-up Letter to a Cordial Interview When Applicant Did Not Get the Job, but Is Asking for Help in Continuing the Job Search

176 South Maple Street
Garden City, New York 11530
April 30, 1995

Mrs. Judith Royce
Zenith Credit Corporation
600 Mulberry Street
Garden City, New York 11529

Dear Mrs. Royce:

I am very sorry I was not the final candidate for the paralegal position at Zenith Credit Corporation. However, I wanted to let you know how much I enjoyed meeting you and thank you for all the time you spent in discussing career opportunities in the paralegal department.

Should you hear of any positions that become available and seem to suit my background and experience, I would appreciate hearing from you. Again, many thanks for your interest.

Sincerely yours,

Ruth Martin

Follow-up Letter to an Informational Interview

5643 Riverside Drive
Berwyn, Illinois 60402
September 8,1995

Mr. Dean McVey
McVey Legal Associates
555 Wacker Drive
Chicago, Illinois 60601

Dear Mr. McVey:

I appreciate the time you took from your busy schedule to discuss future job opportunities as a paralegal with McVey Legal Associates. After our brief meeting, I realized what a good match my skills would be with your firm. I appreciate your interest and helpful suggestions about paralegal career opportunities in general. Should an opening occur within your firm, please keep me in mind.

Again, thank you for your ideas and encouragement. I hope we have an opportunity to meet again.

Sincerely yours,

Andrew Jefferson

Whenever you spend any time with the professional staff of an organization, a follow-up letter is a way of saying "thank you." In the following chapter, we will explore ways in which you can develop your job contacts, expand your networking contacts, and utilize all resources available to you in your job search campaign.

All the exercises you have completed thus far, including the self-assessment and self-evaluation and job search strategies, will serve you well as you move ahead. You have developed tools and tactics. Now you must prepare a well-thought-out strategy. Otherwise, you may easily become frustrated or disillusioned. So how do you begin?

The next chapters will help you structure your job search plan to include all the steps we have covered so far as well as additional steps you will need to take.

8

Your Job Search Plan: Objectives, Resources, Networking, and Record Keeping

The previous chapters of this book have helped you to think about what you have to offer an employer and how to do the paper work, including your skills assessment, resumé, and cover letter—all in preparation for the interview. But unless you have a strategy for finding job opportunities, all that work will not help you. Your job search plan is essential for you to find the best job for you.

Your job search plan should include the following:

1. Your job objectives,
2. Your resources and networking contacts, and
3. Your record-keeping.

Your Job Objectives

What type of employer are you looking for? Include the size of the organization, its location, the type of work specialty (if relevant), and any other details that help you to focus on the kind of job you would like to have. It is not essential for you to limit your options, but the clearer you are in your objectives, the easier it is for you to make a job search plan.

This part of your job search plan should include a list of organizations, firms, and agencies you want to contact for openings. In addition to the name of the firm, list any name or names of persons you can use to contact directly. In your research, you may discover specialties or interests which appeal to you. Review the paralegal specialties in Chapter 2 of this book. In addition, consult the materials, including the list of paralegal employers, in Appendix A for additional information.

Your Job Resources

List all reference materials you plan to use (see Appendix A).

List personal contacts you plan to use. Develop a network. Discussion on network follows.

> *Everyone* you know should be aware that you are looking for a job. The discussion on networking that follows explains how you can widen your range of contacts, but begin by listing all your friends, relatives, and friends of relatives who might be able to help you.

Other job sources should include the following:

Alumni offices, career centers, and job placement offices of schools you have attended

Alumni newsletters

Local bulletin boards and professional newsletters of community and civic organizations

Job fairs

Professional association meetings

Yellow pages

Classified ads

The "hidden job market," opportunities that exist but are not advertised (for example, openings resulting from a merger, expansion, or someone leaving). The best inside track to the hidden job market is through networking.

Add your other job sources to this list.

Using Employment Agencies To Find a Job

Should you use an employment agency to find a job? Recently, a number of employment agencies opened to primarily handle paralegal placement.

Check the yellow pages as well as the classified ads in professional journals. Make certain that the agency does not view paralegals as secretaries with a little extra training. Also, read any agency contract before signing it, so that you understand the fees involved. The best agency reference will be someone who has used and been satisfied with the services of the agency. Agencies that handle temporary job placement might also be a good place for beginners while they search for a job.

In addition to all of the suggestions offered above and in the Job Search Notebook in Appendix B, it is important to understand the concept of networking as a major resource of job opportunities.

Your Networking Resources

In recent years, the concept of networking has become increasingly popular as it relates to job finding, career counseling, and support systems. To understand how networking operates, visualize a series of linkages or connections that leads to other connections. That's what networking is all about: developing connections or contacts who might be able to open some doors for you in your job search.

You are probably familiar with the system referred to as the "old boys' network," in which job information is shared over lunch, on the golf course, or at a party. It's an informal way of discussing what's going on from an insider's vantage point before such information is available to the general public. It's also a system of strategies whereby someone who knows a person within an organization can make a phone call or set up an introduction for you.

When you think of it, each person is the core of a network of friends or associates. In your job search, you must learn how to expand your network. You can do this in a number of ways. Just remember that the focus of your networking should be on the *quality* of your contacts.

How Networking Works

1. Attend professional association meetings. Find out what is going on in the field. In addition to job information, what are the working conditions like in a company? What are the promotion practices? What are current salary ranges?

It takes energy and effort to attend such meetings or job fairs, lectures, or special programs, but the investment of your time is well worth it. You must learn how to put yourself forward, strike up a conversation, or simply listen until you have something to contribute. As you develop a rapport and trust with others, information that is not otherwise discussed becomes easier to talk about and share.

2. Be prepared to deliver a thirty-second commercial on yourself at all times. You might bump into someone at a social function, in an elevator, or waiting in line any place. It's not appropriate, nor do you have the time, to give a lengthy explanation of your job search, but you can briefly mention what you are doing and what you're looking for.

3. Always carry a business card, even if you do not have a job. It is the most efficient and most professional way to give a contact your name and phone number.

4. Networking can take the shape of a casual lunch in which you meet a new person, a friend of a mutual friend. It can take place at a formal party or picnic. All of these occasions provide opportunities for you to develop and expand your connections. If you are not convinced, just take time at a social gathering to watch how people congregate to talk about work-related issues and problems. Work is frequently the common denominator in a discussion, and it is frequently what brings people together, even socially. Observe how others use networking as an effective strategy, and then learn how to use it yourself.

Following Up on Networking Connections

It's important to remember, however, that networking is *not* manipulation or using other people. Everyone must gain something from it; otherwise, it does not work. Below are some suggestions on how to follow through on a networking connection.

1. Once you have made a contact, either in person or on the telephone, ask when would be a convenient time for you to meet the person or to talk. If you've met the person at a social gathering, give the person your business card, if appropriate, at that time or ask if you might call the person within the next few days to continue the conversation. And then be sure to do so soon after the initial meeting; otherwise, you will have to spend time refreshing that person's memory about you.

No matter how you make the contact, there are some professional guidelines to follow in developing this relationship. This applies in all cases: if you have been introduced socially, if the contact is a friend, or if the person is someone who has been referred to you by a mutual friend.

2. Never ask, "Can I have a job?" "Do you have any contacts I can use?" Of course, you hope that information will be offered to you.

3. Never invent connections or refer to a mutual friend if that person has not authorized you to make the contact.

4. Once you have set up a time to talk, make certain that you are focused in what you want to find out. Are you looking for information about the daily responsibilities of a specific job? Do you want to know how the organization views women or whether it encourages continuing education? The more specific you can be, the more useful the contact can be. Personal chitchat can be time consuming. Keep in mind that you are using a person's valuable time.

Reciprocating for Networking Favors

Networking is one of the best ways to find a job, but in order for it to work, it must be viewed as mutually beneficial to the persons involved. No one likes to feel used. Therefore, you must acknowledge and, in some way, reciprocate for the advice or additional contacts offered to you. How do you do this?

1. Always send an acknowledgement letter, thanking those who have given you their time and professional advice. Sample letters are included in this chapter.

2. When you find a job, always write a note informing everyone who has helped you in any way, even if the job did not result from the specific contact. Your professional courtesy will be remembered.

3. Share *your* knowledge, expertise, or current information with any networking contacts. It could simply be a notice of a meeting, lecture, or program that might interest that person or it could be an article or announcement relevant to that person's own job or professional activities. Gifts or anything of monetary value is inappropriate; however, the gesture you make is important. It demonstrates that you also share professional information.

How to Continue Networking Once You Have a Job

Networking on your job or in the professional world at large can be one of the most rewarding ways to move ahead if you are aware that it is not an entitlement. Make it work for you by nurturing your contacts throughout your career.

You can do this in the following ways:

1. Become active in professional or civic groups. One of the best ways to achieve distinction is to donate your time on special projects or assume a leadership role in an organization.

2. Meet with professional colleagues on a regular basis for lunch or dinner to talk about job and career issues and goals. They will also be a good resource for job information.

3. Be generous: Send congratulatory notes to those who have been promoted or have received special recognition or awards. Share information and your knowledge. If you have a reputation as someone who always takes and rarely gives back, your networking efforts will rarely be successful.

Networking will not get you the job, but it will expand your professional circle and it could help you meet the right person.

To help you keep track of your networking contacts, keep a job contact log. A sample log is included here, as well as follow-up thank you letters. Customize them to fit your own situation, and be certain to keep copies of your letters for your files.

Job Contact Log

Name of Firm Address and Phone Number	Action Taken or Results	Date of Follow-up Thank You Letter

Follow-up Thank You Letter

2210 North Wilton Ave.
Chicago, Illinois 60657
September 12, 1995

Ms. Sandra Van Hart
Winston, Bache and Barton
212 West Wacker Drive
Chicago, Illinois 60607

Dear Sandra:

Thank you so much for your valuable time and ideas concerning my job search
as a paralegal and career opportunities in the current job market. I am eager to follow
through on your suggestions and will keep you informed of my progress.

I hope that you are planning to attend the next monthly meeting of the Illinois
Paralegal Association. Judge Amanda Arnold is speaking on "Ethical Responsibilities
and New Paralegal Opportunities." It looks like a good session, and I hope to see you
there.

Thank you, again.

Sincerely yours,

Marion Wilbur

Follow-up to Letter to Someone Who Has Provided a Job Lead

761 Sheridan Avenue
Pittsburgh, Pennsylvania 15202
May 31, 1995

Ms. Adrienne Atkins
Loebig and Loebig
1800 Grant Street
Pittsburgh, Pennsylvania 15202

Dear Ms. Atkins:

Thank you for your ideas and helpful suggestions regarding my search for a paralegal position. At your suggestion, I called John Andrews at Negherbon and Nolton Associates to discuss job possibilities. He was not only cordial, but he invited me to meet with him to discuss expansion plans for his paralegal staff.

Our meeting went very well, and he indicated he would call me when the firm makes its expansion decisions.

I will certainly keep you informed about the outcome. Again, I appreciate your time, interest, and suggestions.

Sincerely yours,

Carole Cartwright

Your Record Keeping System

It is important for you to keep records of every phase of your job campaign; this is not only important in terms of expenses incurred, but doing so will enable you to see what you have accomplished as well as what you need to do. Without a written record, it is sometimes difficult to remember whether or not you sent a follow-up letter. If you list dates, you will also see when a first interview occurred, so that you can time a follow-up phone call if you have not heard anything.

Appendix B includes sample charts to help you with your record keeping as part of your job search plan. These include **Job Listings, Job Interview Logs, Job Contact Logs, Contact List:Address & Phone Numbers, Telephone and Correspondence Log, Expense Records.**

You may also find that keeping a computer record of your job search plan will be most efficient for you.

A **Job Search Checklist** will help you to keep track of your progress. The following chart may serve that purpose. Other charts and checklists in Appendix B of this book will also be helpful.

Job Search Checklist

❐ *Objectives*
  ❐ Type of job (specialty preferred, if any)
  ❐ Location
  ❐ Company size
  ❐ Other preferences in job

❐ *Resources*
  ❐ References used
  ❐ Contacts (personal or professional)

❐ *Record Keeping*
  ❐ Job contact logs
  ❐ Letters sent (with dates)
  ❐ Expense sheets

Freelancing as a Paralegal

You may have thought about freelancing as a paralegal. The following chapter discusses what you need to know about that career option, if and when you decide to pursue that route.

Beyond Beginner: Freelancing as a Paralegal

Many paralegals, once they gain experience and establish a reputation for reliability and professional work, consider freelancing, which involves working as an independent contractor or with other paralegals as part of a group. Before examining ways in which you can follow this path, it is extremely important to understand what a paralegal can and cannot do. For that reason, a discussion of the ethical responsibilities of paralegals is essential before any other consideration.

Ethical Responsibilities of Paralegals

In their book *Legal Ethics for Paralegals and the Law Office* (West Publishing Company, 1995) Laura Morrison and Gina DeCiani present a clear, thorough understanding of the legal limitations of paralegals. It is crucial to remember that paralegals are not attorneys; even as freelancers they cannot practice law. They must work under the supervision of a lawyer. A paralegal's client is one to whom *paralegal* services are offered, not *legal* services.

There are certain areas, therefore, that must be handled very carefully, including depositions, court appearances, pleadings, and the offering of any kind of legal advice. A problem arises when exceptions occur. For example, in some local jurisdictions, paralegals may represent their lawyer-employer in court if the case is uncontested. Such exceptions may set a precedent for other jurisdictions; however, the basic rule remains the same. Paralegals cannot represent clients in court.

Paralegals may be present at depositions, but a lawyer must conduct the deposition. Paralegals assist lawyers and, in many cases, are factual experts as a result of their extensive research on any given case; legally, however, they cannot answer questions or give legal advice.

They cannot sign a pleading, which constitutes a written court appearance, or any other document filed in court on the client's behalf.

Here are some basic points to keep in mind:

1. Avoid conflict-of-interest situations. If you work for several law firms that specialize in the same area, you may find that you are working for opposing sides of a case. If you are uncertain what to do about this, ask the attorneys for whom you will be working whether they feel that your working for both clients would constitute a conflict. If so, it is your ethical responsibility to act accordingly, particularly if you are working in a litigation case.

2. While your duties and responsibilities are diverse, you must remember that paralegals are not lawyers, and that you may not give legal advice to a nonlawyer client, may not represent a client in court, and may not advertise your services as those of a lawyer.

In order to protect yourself from any possibility of infringement of these laws, it is best to take some precautions by following these guidelines:

1. Never work directly for the public. Always work for an attorney.

2. Do not meet independently with a client of an attorney.

3. Make certain that the attorney for whom you are working reviews and signs your work.

4. Have the attorney for whom you are working give you a letter that authorizes you to perform certain duties for him or her.

5. Be certain that the attorney for whom you are working has been admitted to practice law in your state.

These guidelines are easier to follow when you work under the direct supervision of an attorney; as a freelancer, however, it important to remember these distinctions.

In Appendix C of this book the codes of ethics and professional responsibility of the National Association of Legal Assistants and the National Federation of Paralegal Association are included. They will serve as useful references at all stages of your paralegal career, particularly if you decide to freelance.

In addition to recognizing the legal responsibilities of freelancing, it is important to understand the professional and personal qualifications necessary to succeed and the marketing strategies you must develop as a self-employed paralegal.

Types of Freelance Paralegals

Independent Contractor

There are two types of freelance paralegals. The first is usually referred to as an as an *independent contractor*, or a paralegal who is not on the payroll of any one organization. This type of paralegal works independently and bills his or her services to an attorney or law firm. Independent contractors usually bill on an hourly basis but at times will contract for a specific project or a fixed rate for the entire project.

Frequently, independent contractor paralegals work out of their homes and provide services in many areas of legal practice. They often use a post office box address to maintain their professional image.

Service-Group Paralegal

The second type of freelance paralegal is known as a *service-group paralegal,* or one who works as part of a service company. Paralegal service companies usually have their own office space, have a staff of clerical help, and may offer specialized services, as in trust and estate law. Essentially, these groups are made up of entrepreneurs who need to be good business managers as well as knowledgeable paralegals. Unsuspecting paralegals may become victims to vendors, without legal qualifications, who try to sell franchises for running a paralegal service company. This point underscores the earlier recommendation that only experienced paralegals consider freelancing as a career option. They will know the questions to ask and will have developed professional contacts in the field to rely on when making such a decision.

In addition to ethical considerations, there are other major issues to consider before embarking on your career as a freelance paralegal. You must ask yourself whether you have the right qualifications.

Qualifications

To be qualified to offer paralegal services, you need credentials and experience. Only with training and professional experience will you gain the necessary expertise to convince a client to buy your services. That client will want to know your background, what you have done, and how your former clients feel about your work. For these reasons, freelancing is not a sound career path for the beginning paralegal. After several years, you will have gained the experience to handle complex tasks; routine tasks require less experience. But your overall judgment as a paralegal will improve with experience, and your goal must be to sell your client first-rate paralegal services. If you establish a reputation as a careless, inexperienced paralegal your freelancing career will never get off the ground.

If you gain experience by working under the direct supervision of an attorney before becoming a freelancer, you will not only develop a certain expertise but you will have developed a level of self-confidence necessary to get started on your own.

In addition to the professional qualifications, you will need certain personal qualifications for success as a freelance paralegal. Most of these traits are the same ones necessary for any entrepreneur who wants to succeed in business:

1. You must be committed to working long, irregular hours.

2. You must have strong interpersonal communication skills.

3. You must be able to work under varying deadlines

4. You must be able to handle pressure.

5. You must be a self-motivated, self-directed person.

6. You must have good time management skills.

7. You must have a strong business sense.

8. You must have energy, persistence, and drive.

Remember that your first clients are the ones who will help you to establish your reputation. You cannot afford to be anything less than punctual and completely accurate in the work you do. While these traits are important in any job, as an independent paralegal, you will never hold clients or gain new ones if your reputation is not built on these factors.

How much start-up money will you need? Certain investments will have to be made, even in the early stages of freelancing, if you hope to succeed. You should have a personal computer, a separate business phone line, a fax machine, business cards, and business stationery. You should subscribe to WESTLAW or LEXIS/NEXIS. These are basics. Later on, you may wish to develop a brochure or other marketing materials. Speak to other paralegals who are freelancing or have done so in the past. You can do this at professional meetings. Even though other paralegals may be potential competitors, in the early stages of your freelancing, you will not pose a threat to them. And if you have developed your networking resources, these contacts will come in very handy before you embark on your entrepreneurial career. You may be able to save time and money and avoid a lot of headaches.

Many freelancers work part time for someone else until they develop their own clientele. And this raises a very important issue which we will address later: conflict of interests.

A final qualification that will serve you well as a freelancer is development of your selling skills. You are selling a service, as well as yourself. But in order for someone to buy your product, you must know how to present it. A good speaking or presentation skills course and constant practice will prove very helpful to you, particularly before you approach your first clients. One way to gain such experience is to give speeches before any audience, including paralegal and other professional associations, and civic and church groups. If you choose a topic that interests you as well as the group, you have an enthusiasm for your topic. You will also be developing self-confidence, interacting with the public, learning to overcome your weaknesses, and, at the same time, developing an identity within the community. It will require a commitment of your time and energy, but you will gain valuable experience that will help you later on.

In a competitive marketplace, you also gain the edge over other freelancing paralegals if you develop a specialty and gain as much as experience as you can in it. In doing so, you develop a reputation as a qualified, skilled paralegal and build your clientele by good, strong referrals.

How Will You Get Started?

Once you identify your special skills and talents and order your business cards and stationery, you must make a plan for marketing your services. This means doing your homework!

The art of selling your services as a paralegal is to know the needs of your clients and convince them that you can meet those needs. They must also recognize that you can save them time and money; you offer them convenience and value. Some of the following guidelines may help you to get started.

1. *List your particular skills and specialties.* What specific tasks can you perform and what experience have you had that will demonstrate your abilities in these areas? Remember that any employer is always looking for skills and accomplishments. Although you may be self-employed, every client is a new employer.

2. *Identify your prospective clients.* Evaluate how they could use your services to save them time and money. For example, could they use someone skilled in a particular area at a particular time of year or for a specific project? You have to convince them that it is in their best interest to contract individually for these jobs, rather than to hire a full-time

person or use their own in-house staff that could, perhaps, use their time and talents in other areas, in a more productive way. In other words, you must prove to them that you are cost effective.

3. *Focus on your specific personal and professional skills by listing them*. This stage is important as a preliminary step for your marketing literature.

4. *Plan a brochure*. While this step may seem costly and you may not want to initially invest money in a printed brochure, think about what you would like to include. Eventually, a brochure will be an important part of your marketing strategy.

   A good brochure need not be complicated; as a matter of fact, it should be clear and direct so that a potential client can easily see what you have to offer. Be brief and specific, and include all essential information, such as your name, address, phone number, and fax number. As you develop a client list, you may want to include that list (with permission of the clients, of course), as well as any comments or quotations from clients, in your brochure.

   To keep costs down, make your brochure a one-page brochure that can be folded for mailing purposes and easier reading. Avoid distracting graphics; you project a more professional image if you keep your lettering simple and your copy basic. You can always give additional information and details when you meet a client in person. A brochure should be an invitation to find out more about you and your services. Remember: In many cases this will be your professional introduction, so make certain that it looks absolutely professional in every way, including professional printing.

   Take the time to review sample brochures that most printers have available. While you can get started as a freelancer without a brochure, you will market your services with greater ease if you have some printed material to explain what you do. For mailing purposes, a brochure enclosed with a letter makes your selling job much easier.

5. *Order business cards and stationery with your letterhead*. If you cannot afford the services of a graphic artist, a good printer can help you with a professional logo or design.

6. *Successful marketing is ultimately a matter of numbers*. For every hundred letters or phone calls you make, you may receive only a few responses. In the beginning, you have to develop a reputation. This requires patience on your part; it also requires that you spend time following through or calling back potential clients.

Where do you find these clients? Every organization, whatever its size, is a potential client base if it has a need for the services of a paralegal. You might feel that small, independent practitioners or companies would be your most likely clientele. That is not necessarily the situation. Many larger firms do have in-house staff, but at certain times, with specific projects, they may have too much work for their regular staff and would welcome the services of a freelance paralegal, particularly one with the specialty they need.

To let potential clients know about your services, you must advertise what you have to offer. This does not mean expensive advertising, particularly in the beginning. You can place ads in legal newspapers under "legal services"; this will attract the attention of a population that you want to reach—the attorneys in your city or town. Other inexpensive means of advertising include listing your services on the bulletin boards of your local bar association, if permissible, and in newsletters, and having your brochures available for distribution at any large gathering of professionals who could use your services.

Whatever the marketing plan you develop, remember that it is essential for you to follow up on everyone who expresses an interest in your services. Keep a record or log, along with the dates of your meetings, letters, or phone calls. If you are to be successful as a freelance paralegal, potential clients must know who you are and what you can do for them. In other words, you must find ways to gain visibility so that attorneys will have you in mind when they need the services of a freelance paralegal.

Other Important Considerations

There are other important issues to consider when planning your career as a freelance paralegal.

Getting Paid

As a freelancer, you must learn how and when to bill your clients. One of the most difficult aspects of working for yourself is collecting money for services you have performed. For that reason, it is essential that you remember some basic points:

1. Explain your fees to your clients and make certain that you agree upon what your reimbursement will be. Confirm this agreement in writing, so there is no dispute later on or any confusion about the terms you have stipulated.

2. Whether you decide to bill on an hourly basis (and you can check either in your community or with your local paralegal association to find out the going rate) or charge a flat fee for a specific project, be certain to bill your clients promptly. For lengthy projects, it is wise to bill regularly, every week or two. For a shorter project, send your bill within two weeks of completion of your work.

Unfortunately, no matter how well you plan and set up agreements, there will always be clients with whom you will have problems in collecting your fee, so you must plan for certain losses as a freelancer. You will come to identify and avoid working with such clients.

Remaining Professional and Avoiding Conflicts of Interest

Review the opening paragraphs of this chapter that discuss the ethical responsibilities of being a freelance paralegal. This issue is so important that you must always review your plans and actions to make certain that you are not overstepping your boundaries as a paralegal. Your practice, your professionalism, and your future as a paralegal are at stake.

Keep abreast of problems that have faced other other freelance paralegals, and learn how they have solved them. Become familiar with your local paralegal association, not only to learn about job opportunities which may exist, but also to find out how to enhance your professional status as a paralegal within the community, whether you decide to work independently, as a freelancer, or within an organization as a full-time paralegal.

Finally, here are some helpful hints and suggestions on becoming a successful freelancer from Jean Hellman, Director of the Institute for Paralegal Studies at Loyola University Chicago.

1. *It is essential to keep accurate, up-to-date records of all income and expenses.* Formal bookkeeping isn't required, but you must have a system. Keep your check stubs or make copies of paychecks before depositing them. Collect receipts for all supplies, materials and equipment. *Have a separate checking account for your business; it is also good idea to have a separate phone line if you are working from your home.*

2. *Consider the legal aspects of doing business on your own.* If you are asked to sign a contract, read it carefully and make sure you understand every word before signing. If you're uncertain, get legal advice; it shouldn't cost much and will be well worth it in preventing problems later on.

3. *Understand the tax consequences of freelancing.* If your employer is not withholding taxes, you may have to make estimated tax payments quarterly and pay Social Security taxes when you file your annual return. If you don't, you may be penalized by the Internal Revenue Service. Again, tax advice is relatively inexpensive. A good tax advisor will also be able to tell you of deductions you may take against your business income (even under new tax laws). This is another reason why your record keeping is so important.

While freelancing as a paralegal may appear to be complicated, the rewards can be great. Only you can decide on the route you wish to follow.

As in any decision, the more you understand about the implications and the consequences, the easier it may be for you to choose the best option for you.

In order to make the maximum use of your time and monetary investment, you need to establish efficient systems for your calendar, billing, telephones, filing, references, and resources. The following checklist may be helpful in the beginning.

Sample Checklist for Freelancing

(You may wish to duplicate this for monthly items.)

Expense Sheet

Item	Amount	Date
Stationery		
Business Cards		
Contracts		
Postage		
Supplies (list)		
Travel Expenses		
Telephone		
Office Equipment (list)		
Professional Dues/Memberships		
Other		

Income Sheet

Received From	Payment For	Date	Amount	Balance Due

10

Paralegal: Stepping Stone to Other Careers

As you begin your career as a paralegal, you will probably not be interested in seeing how your training can prepare you for jobs and careers outside the legal field. Sometime later, however, you might find such information useful. It is very helpful therefore, to consider these options as your career progresses, even from the beginning. For you will realize that your education and training as a paralegal may well serve as a stepping stone to other areas that may be of interest to you.

In the beginning of this book, we discussed what it takes to become a successful paralegal. Many of the qualifications listed are the same ones necessary for success in several other fields or professions. With the professional training of a paralegal, you may wish to explore some of these fields once you gain some experience.

Many of you may have trained in other fields before becoming a paralegal. As a matter of fact, one of the problems many people face as they begin this new career is how to explain what might be a radical career change to a potential employer. If you can learn how to build on your skills developed in another field and relate these skills to your paralegal training, then you will benefit from the broad range of your talents and experiences, rather than be at a disadvantage.

Eventually, you may find that you can use this combination of skills and training if you wish to move on to another field. Consider the following examples:

1. Depending upon your specific interests and talents, you can make many moves within the paralegal profession, as well as outside of it.

2. Management skills could enable you to become a paralegal coordinator, one who trains and supervises other paralegals within an organization. The best route to this position is to demonstrate your capabilities, and you can do this only within the organization itself.

3. Office management is another area in which you can use your management supervisory skills, if you have them. This could be within a legal firm, or once you have gained experience, you may find that many offices need good management, outside as well as inside the legal profession.

4. Administration within a legal firm is also based on strong skills in working with personnel of many departments. An administrative director of a law firm is usually responsible for every nonlegal aspect of the firm's operation, including accounting, personnel, and purchasing. Remember that such a position is not a paralegal position, although your paralegal background will be helpful. It is a step onto a different career track, however.

This person usually reports to a senior officer. It is a highly responsible and demanding position. The combination of paralegal skills and other administrative skills could lead to a rewarding and challenging position.

Within large and small, nonprofit and corporate environments, paralegals have many opportunities open to them. Even if you decide that you do not wish to pursue any of these options at this stage of your career, knowing about them will help you to focus on where you might want to be five or ten years in the future. By thinking of your long-term goals, you can develop skills along the way that will enable you to achieve your goals.

Here are some opportunities you might want to consider:

1. *Computer center specialist or manager:* Computer literacy training, in addition to specialized or generalist paralegal training, could make you a suitable candidate for a position as a computer center manager. While duties may vary, they would include working with information systems, electronic data banks, and word processing. In today's job market, you will need computer skills to work as a paralegal. This could be a very satisfying career alternative for anyone interested in working in the computer field.

2. *Law librarian:* Law firms usually hire law librarians to handle their periodical collections, as well as law books and manuals. Although many of these law positions are filled by those with library training, frequently a paralegal with a good academic background can be trained to fill this position.

3. *Social service agent:* This area is extremely appropriate for anyone interested in the social welfare system, the criminal justice system, or immigration services, just to name a few. Many positions offered are not

listed as paralegal positions, but a review of the job description and responsibilities reveals that employees are essentially doing paralegal work, in addition to other duties. For example, a position within a social service organization that assists immigrants may be listed as "Immigrant Specialist." That person may serve as an advocate for immigrants in court and may have great deal of interaction with clients but, for the most part, the skills required for this position are basically those required to be a paralegal. Many social service agencies have such positions. It is important, therefore, to read the job description and qualifications necessary, if you are interested in moving into this field.

4. *Educator:* Teacher, program administrator, consultant, education coordinator for continuing legal education are examples of areas open to paralegals in the field of education. Check with local universities, colleges, and community colleges for requirements.Many schools are interested in hiring part-time faculty to teach an occasional course. This could be an opportunity for you to see if you would like to work in the academic world.

5. *Banking specialist:* In addition to work as a paralegal in a bank, other opportunities exist, particularly with the new and changing regulations for foreign as well as domestic banking. If you are interested in working in this environment, your best path would be to begin working as a paralegal to discover options that exist and develop a network to help you find out about openings as they occur.

   Other careers involving money and banking include importing and exporting and stock brokerage. These fields may require additional credentials or particular qualifications.

6. *Government specialist:* Many paralegals are interested in government regulatory issues; politics or working in a political environment can always be explored; lobbying is a career for which paralegals could be well suited. In addition, civil service opportunities are available. Check your local government offices along, with times and dates of civil service examinations.

7. *Journalist:* Research and writing in the legal field is a career open to those who have demonstrated their writing skills and expertise in a field or specialty. While many may wish to pursue this goal on a freelance basis, there are companies which hire paralegals and then use their writing talents predominantly.

8. *Salesperson:* Those interested in combining interpersonal skills and and paralegal training with a personal need to receive the rewards of their individual efforts, may consider sales, specifically for all materials and equipment used by attorneys.

9. *Corporate specialist:* Review the paralegal specialties listed in the first chapter of this book to give you some idea of particular specialties. Developing experience or expertise in those areas will prepare you for

many types of work within a corporation. Some of these areas include working in the patent or trademark division or employee benefits office.

10. *Real estate specialist:* You may develop a paralegal specialty in this area and work with an attorney in various aspects when you realize that you enjoy the real estate field and all of its possibilities. As a result, you may think of real estate sales or management, including title and mortgage company positions. Your paralegal training will be an additional asset.

11. *Medical specialist:* With changing policies regarding health care in this country, many career options exist in this field for paralegals. Within hospital settings or insurance agencies (even nonmedical insurance firms), your paralegal training will prepare you to take on additional responsibilities if you have the other personal and professional qualifications.

While each of these fields might require additional training (not necessarily a degree, but some specialized training that could be gained on the job), they should be considered, particularly if they seem to tie in with your interests, talents, and goals.

You may, of course, plan to go on to law school, but the point of this discussion is to emphasize that becoming a paralegal can lead you to job opportunities in many different fields that are directly related or indirectly related to the legal field.

Additional educational training might be necessary should you wish to become an expert in the field. That may not always be the case, however. For example, you may not be certain where your true interests and talents lie, so until you know this, going ahead with additional education or training may not be the answer. Being a paralegal will give you a good idea of what it would be like to remain in the legal field should you decide you want to become a lawyer. But even if you do not wish to do so, think of your paralegal training as a background for developing other interests you have. It's also important to realize that being a paralegal could easily be a stepping stone to other careers that are not as rigorous or demanding as that of a paralegal—or perhaps even more so, but in a different way. There may be other areas in which you could expand your talents and professional options.

In considering your professional development as a paralegal or in other fields, review the list of resources in Appendix A of this book, talk to people who have used their paralegal background and try to determine which areas or professions hold a particular appeal for you. Learn to ask questions and look for opportunities as you make your plans.

Suggestions for Planning Your Future as a Paralegal

1. Develop special interests and expertise in the area of law that appeals to you.

2. Continue your professional education. Become involved with your local paralegal association. Attend professional workshops and programs that will help you develop your skills and inform you about options.

3. Develop your networking affiliations. Let people know of your interests and ambitions. Don't forget to thank them when they have helped you in any way.

4. Look for ways to become the best at what you do and gain visibility for your work.

5. Remember that you should at least perform the job for which you are hired. If you become bored or burned out, it could be that you have not planned to take the next step. Always keep in mind that you do have options. Discover them.

6. Update your resumé periodically. Be prepared to submit a copy to someone who could be interested in what you have done.

7. Learn to build on your past experiences and integrate them into the job you are doing that relates to a position you would like to have.

8. Take the time and effort to develop strong communication skills: interpersonal, written, and verbal.

9. Find ways to use these skills so that you are recognized not only for what you do, but for what you are capable of doing.

10. Learn to set standards of excellence for yourself in your job without being a fanatic perfectionist or judging the work of others. Know the job for which you are responsible, and do it to the best of your ability.

11. Develop a self-analytical approach to your job and yourself. In planning your future, determine what is important to you as a professional, learn to examine your options carefully, and learn what steps you will need to take for you to achieve your goals.

11

On the Job: The First Thirty Days

The purpose of this section is to walk you through the first thirty days of your new job as a paralegal. It describes what happens once you are hired and walk through the door, based on actual accounts of people who have been there.

Most of your time and energy up until this point has been devoted to the job search and all the tasks that are required. Once you have a job, you can begin to think about what you will be doing when you start working. You may understandably have questions about the job and the organization, concerns about your capabilities and overwhelming anxieties about starting a new position.

This chapter includes many questions that other paralegals have asked or wish they had asked as they began working. Some may seem obvious, and others may not have occurred to you. You may wonder where to begin asking. The questions included here are general in nature. Responses to these questions and additional advice from paralegals are also given. Obviously, each job is unique and each new paralegal will have questions about his or her particular situation. Add your own questions, issues, and concerns to those raised in this chapter.

As you think about your questions and concerns and read these personal accounts, the anxiety you feel about your first days at work will probably lessen. Remember to rely on the same principles you used in the job search: The better prepared you are, the more successful you are likely to be.

Think of this chapter, then, as a step-by-step guide to becoming a successful paralegal once you *have* a job.

Questions to Ask Before the First Day

- What time should you start work?
- What is the exact location to which you should report?
- What is the name of the person to whom you should report?

Before the first day of work, be sure you know the answers to the above questions. When you leave for work, allow enough time to arrive early. It is not proper to be early for an interview, but you don't need to be afraid to be too early for work. You cannot afford to be late. Excuses are not acceptable. If you know that a train or bus sometimes runs late, take an earlier one. If you will be driving during rush hour, allow plenty of time to make the trip and to find a place to park.

Remember that your demeanor on the first day of work is the first impression you will make on your colleagues. They will expect you to be a bit nervous, but if you are late, you will make a negative impression, and in the early stages of the new job, you want to do everything you can to create a positive impression. Initial impressions are very important, so make every effort to make a positive one by what you say and how you behave.

Questions to Ask as You Begin Working

Some information is essential for you to know when you start a new job. This is the time to ask all the questions you need to ask to clarify your position. The other employees will expect you to ask questions. If you have thought through these questions before you begin working, you will not have to interrupt anyone over and over. If you do not understand the answers, now is the time to clarify any confusion about your duties or responsibilities. You will not be faulted for asking questions, many questions, especially in the beginning. You will be responsible for knowing the answers to important questions, particularly as you gain experience on the job. It is up to you to find out where to get these answers.

1. *Find out where things are:*
   - What is the layout of the office?
   - Where are the attorneys' offices, especially the attorneys with whom you will be working?
   - Where are the washrooms and lunchrooms?
   - Where are the most convenient restaurants?
   - Where is the best place to park?

2. *Find out about office policies and procedures:*

   - How is the payroll handled?

   - What deductions will be taken out of your paycheck?

   - What forms do you need to fill out?

   - What is the policy on sick days and emergencies?

   - What insurance benefits are you entitled to receive?

3. *Find out about your supervisor and work assignments:*

   - Who are the attorneys with whom you will be working? (Find their offices and introduce yourself.)

   - Who is your immediate supervisor?

   - Who will be giving you work assignments?

   - Who is the best person to talk to when you have questions about your work?

4. *Find out about policies regarding confidentiality:*

   - What are the guidelines on confidentiality?

   - Can files be taken out of the office if you want to work on them at home?

   - What can or cannot be discussed outside the office?

5. *Find out about billing procedures:*

   - What is the billing procedure for time and materials, including photo-copying materials and phone calls?

   - Are these expenses billed to the client?

   - If so, is there a billing code that should be used?

6. *Find out about support services:*

   - Where are the offices of the secretarial and other support staff?

   - Are you entitled to ask for clerical assistance?

7. *Find out about office supplies:*

   - Where are the office supplies kept?

   - What is the procedure for requisitioning supplies?

   - How do the photocopying and fax machines work?

   - Who do you ask for assistance on these matters?

8. *Find out about other things you'd like to know:*

_____

_____

_____

_____

Many other questions will arise once you begin working. Try to identify a reliable person and ask if it is all right to consult with him or her when you have a question.

A Word About the Support Staff

Learning to work with the support staff is extremely important! They can be immensely helpful to you. They usually know everything there is to know about office procedures and protocol. Respect them, and don't forget to thank them for any assistance they give you.

In a large organization, the secretary or secretarial staff may work for several attorneys. Take into consideration the deadlines of others in the office, and be cooperative in establishing your own deadline. A secretary can be a great ally, so any effort you make to be considerate of his or her situation will eventually pay off.

Questions on Sensitive Issues (and Advice from Paralegals)

Some questions may be delicate, and they deserve special consideration here. The suggested responses are from experienced paralegals.

- What if you receive one answer to a question during the job interview but a different answer when you start working?

You will have asked many questions during the interview, but the person who interviewed you may not be the person for whom you are working, and you may get different answers to the same question. Your responsibility is to the person for whom you are working. If this causes confusion, it is important that you ask for clarification immediately.

- What if the job you are asked to do is not the job for which you were hired?

If you are asked to work on an assignment for which you are not prepared, it is important for you to ask the right questions. Don't agree immediately to do the assignment, but don't refuse to do it. Write down the instructions exactly. Tell the attorney that you have never handled such an assignment before (the attorney may not be aware of your experience or training) but that you are willing to do it with some guidance. If you don't think you are prepared to handle it, it is far better to be honest about this than to agree to do the assignment and fail. If you give the impression that you are willing to work and learn but are also honest about your skills and abilities, you will be establishing a reputation for reliability and conscientiousness.

- What if you are working for several attorneys and each has an urgent deadline? How do you set priorities?

Learn to say "no" tactfully to a new assignment if you are working to meet a deadline for another attorney. You may tell the second attorney that the new assignment will create a conflict for you because you are working on another assignment with an urgent deadline. At the same time, present another option. Ask if you could do it the next day, or whenever your deadline for the first assignment will have been met. By offering to work on the assignment at a later time, you will not give the impression that you are trying to avoid more work. You will let the attorney know that you are trying to establish a schedule so that you can complete all the assignments you are asked to do.

- What if you are given two assignments simultaneously?

Talk to the appropriate person about which one should have priority. In the early days on the job, there will a great temptation for you to try to do everything to impress your new employer. And while it is important to establish a reputation for conscientiousness, it is just as important to demonstrate how you work with varying deadlines and how well you can set priorities. In order to do this, you must know what is expected of you and understand your employer's priorities. You must find out this information as soon as possible if you are to succeed in your new position.

More Advice From Paralegals

Here are some general comments from paralegals regarding their first days on the job, how they felt, and what they wished they had known.

1. *The most difficult or confusing aspects of my first few days on the job:*
   - I didn't know the organizational structure (the name of the managing partner; the hierarchy of attorneys and support staff).
   - I didn't know the other paralegals. I wish someone had introduced me to them.

- I didn't know where to find supplies.

- I wondered where everything was. A lot of law firms do not give orientations. Some have manuals, but the manuals may be outdated. Ask if your name should be put on a mailing list.

- It was hard to get to know people (peers). You need to make the effort to network. Don't wait to be introduced.

2. *Things I wish I had known or someone had told me:*

   - How to use the phone system.

   - How to address the attorneys in the law firm, whether some or all should be called by their first names.

   - That I had to sign in and out every day.

   - How much clerical work (i.e. typing) I'd have to do.

   - How to dress professionally.

   - How much overtime I'd be working.

   - That if you worked on Saturdays, you were entitled to a free lunch but that your name had to put on a list for this.

   - Exactly what my job duties would be. I would have asked more questions during the interview.

   - Where to find answers and how to find a mentor.

   - When preparing documents, how to date stamp documents and put them in chronological order.

   - That I had been more flexible.

   - That I had listened more and talked less.

3. *Tips on what to avoid:*

   - Don't be too opinionated or critical about the way things are done. You may have some good ideas about improving efficiency, but remember that things have been done a certain way for a specific reason and even "constructive criticisms" may alienate those who have been at the organization for some time.

   - Don't make judgment calls about your work. Ask for advice if you are not sure what to do.

   - Don't be unprofessional in your appearance, behavior, or the manner in which you address others in the organization. If you are not certain how to address someone, ask.

   - Don't make excuses for being late.

- Don't think you must know everything at once. You will be expected to know how to do your job, but it is far better to ask questions than to demonstrate false confidence and make errors.

Planning for the Future

It is never too early to look toward the future, no matter whether you are an entry-level paralegal or an experienced one. Continuing legal education will help you succeed in your job and enable you to move ahead in the profession. These courses or programs, frequently offered as seminars and designed specifically for paralegals, can be extremely valuable. They can help you to develop or update your skills and expertise, or to discover a new area you would like to pursue. Generally, the focus is on current issues and legislation in a particular legal specialty, such as real estate, the environment, intellectual property, consumer fraud, medical malpractice and many others. Check with your local universities or paralegal association for the location and availability of program offerings.

The Excitement and the Challenges of Your New Job

The first days of a new job can be exciting and even a bit overwhelming. Keep in mind that this is the job you worked so hard to get. You have the professional qualifications, training, and personal traits that convinced your employer to hire you. That should give you the self-confidence you need. You now have the opportunity to become the best paralegal you can be. Meet the challenge and enjoy the experience! Good luck!

Appendix A: Resources and Information

In all aspects of your job search, you will need a broad range of information on available resources. The purpose of this Appendix is to help you locate what you need to know in order to become well-informed and well-prepared.

All the information included is current at the time of publication, but be certain to verify specific names, addresses, and phone numbers for any recent changes. Following is an outline of the information you will find in this appendix:

1. Employers of Paralegals

2. Directories
   General
   Banking
   Government
   Insurance
   Corporate
   Probate
   Real Estate
   Legal Aid Organizations

3. Legal Publications

4. Bar Associations

5. Federal Job Information Centers

6. Paralegal Associations in the United States

7. Additional Sources of Job Leads

8. Recommended Reading

Employers of Paralegals

A large percentage of paralegals may choose to work in traditional law firms of varying sizes and with different specialties. Information on how to locate these companies is listed in this Appendix. In addition to these traditional firms which practice law, there are many other opportunities for paralegals who decide to use their skills in other settings.

Following is a list of categories of paralegal employment.

- *Private Law Firms, and legal clinics*
  Paralegal duties
  Office managers
  General legal administrators
- *Businesses*
  Corporations
  Banks and lending institutions
  Accounting firms
  Brokerage firms
  Insurance companies
  Mortgage and title companies
- *Special Interest Groups*
  Consumer affair groups
  Business associations
  Civil Liberties Union
  Labor unions
  Trade associations
  Citizen action groups
  Environmental protection groups
  Taxpayer associations
- *Consulting Firms and Service Organizations*
  Trademark searches
  Billing services
  Branch office establishment
  Computer systems selection
- *Educational Institutions*
  Paralegal programs
  Administration
  Admissions
  Placement

Paralegal training

Internship coordination

Law librarian

- *Government: Civil Service Departments*

Federal government

Office of the chief government lawyer (attorney general, corporation counsel)

General counsel's office of individual agencies

Departments of individual agencies (civil rights division, enforcement department)

State or local government

Offices of state and local politicians (governor, mayor, commissioner, alderman, representative, senator)

Research assistant, legal analyst, administrative aide, investigator, examiner

- *Legal Services or Legal Aid Offices*

Community legal service offices; legal aid offices providing services with the following titles:

Administrative Benefits Representative

Administrative Hearing Representative

AFDC Specialist (Aid to Families with Dependent Children)

Bankruptcy Law Specialist

Case Advocate

Community Education Specialist

Consumer Law Specialist

Disabled, Specialist in the Law of

Domestic Relations Specialist

Employment Law Specialist

Generalist Paralegal

Health Law Specialist

Housing or Tenant Law Specialist

Immigrant Law Specialist

Information and Referral Specialist

Legal Research Specialist

Paralegal Coordinator

Public Entitlement Specialist

Senior Citizen Specialist

Social Security Specialist

Tribal Court Representative

Veterans Law Specialist

Wills Procedures Specialist

Directories

Law directories are available in most states and frequently on the city or county level.

General Directories

American Bar Reference Handbook

The American Law Guide (2 Park Avenue, New York)

Statistical and descriptive information on the top two hundred law firms and major legal centers in the United States, including departments by size and specialty and key clients and cases.

Attorneys and Agents Registered to Practice before the United States Patent and Trademark Office (listed alphabetically by state)

Directory of Directories (Gale Research Company, Detroit)

A reference guide to directories in business, government, and public affairs. Includes useful sections on specific areas, such as finance, banking, and real estate.

Lawyer's Register by Specialties and Field of Law (published annually by the Lawyer to Lawyer Consultation Panel, Inc., Cleveland)

National guide listing attorneys by specialty with a section on corporate legal departments.

Martindale-Hubbell Law Directory (published annually by Martindale-Hubbell, Inc., Summit, New Jersey)

A listing of all attorneys admitted to the state bars in the United States, as well as some foreign attorneys. Listing is by state with three individual sections under each state: (1) attorneys and their law firms; (2) attorneys registered to practice before the United States Patent and Trademark Office; and (3) biographical directory of state law firms, listed by local address, including firm's specialties.

Smaller law firms frequently are not listed in this directory. Check your local yellow pages for information on smaller firms, including their specialties.

Recently, legal assistant information has been added to this directory. This will be a valuable reference for identifying paralegals, including schools they attended as well as their specialties.

Sullivan's Law Directory

Usually available in any law library, this single-volume directory lists all Illinois attorneys who submit an entry, without charge to the attorney. Attorneys are listed under the names of firm by which they are employed (corporations, banks, trust companies, railroads, associations). Some entries list specialty groups within legal departments; government officials are also listed (federal, state, county, city). Although this directory's listings are exclusively in Illinois, other states have similar directories. Ask the reference librarian at the local county library if such a volume is available.

Specialized Directories

Banking Directories

American Bank Attorneys (Capron Publishing Corporation, Wellesley Hills, Massachusetts)

Moody's Directories (Bank and Financial Manual)
Includes a list of over 10,000 banks and financial institutions.

Government Directories

Federal Personnel Office Directory
Lists over 1500 United States Government hiring offices.

Federal Career Opportunities
Practical newsletter with information on how to find a federal job.

Federal Executive Directory Annual

Municipal and County Executive Directory Annual
Lists appointed and elected officials in all levels of local government.

Paralegal's Guide to U.S. Government Jobs: How to Land a Job in 70 Law-Related Careers
Descriptions of federal job occupations suitable for paralegals along with directions for the application process. A listing of federal personnel offices is included.

State Executive Directory Annual

United States Government Manual
Listing of all federal government agencies and commissions with divisions and functions of each. See below for additional information on federal jobs.

Insurance Directories

Best's Recommended Insurance Attorneys (Oldwick, New Jersey)

Hine's Insurance Counsel (Hine's Legal Directory, Inc., Glen Ellyn, Illinois)

The Insurance Bar (Bar List Publishing Co., Northfield, Illinois)

Lists of Lawyers for Motorists (Automobile Legal Association, Wellesley, Massachusetts)

Markham's Negligence Counsel (Markham Publishing Counsel, Stanford, Connecticut)

Motor Club of America Law List for Motorists (Motor Club of America, Newark, New Jersey)

Underwriters List of Trial Counsel (Underwriters List Publication Co., Cincinnati)

Corporate Directories

Directory of Corporate Affiliations: "Who Owns Whom"

Directory of Corporate Counsel (Dun's Marketing Service Books)

Guide to Business: Industrial Manual
Information on companies listed on the New York and American Stock Exchanges.

The Law and Business Directory of Corporate Counsel (Law and Business Inc., Harcourt Brace Jovanovich, New York)
Listing of over 4500 companies, including utility companies, insurance companies, and financial institutions. Names of attorneys, with educational backgrounds, specialty, bar affiliation, and work experience. Geographical index included.

Law Firms Yellow Book
Nationwide directory of general corporate law firms. Lists attorney and administrative personnel.

McMillan Directory of Leading Private Companies
Officers, managers, and general counsel included first by state, then alphabetically.

Million Dollar Directory
Information on over 120,000 businesses with a net worth of over $1,500,000. Geographical and specialty listing.

Standard and Poor's Register of Corporations, Directors, and Executives (The Standard and Poor Company, New York)

Published semimonthly with descriptions of publicly held corporations and their records. Names and titles of each company are listed, with a description of the firm's major services or products. A separate volume lists all American executives, with educational backgrounds. Index categorizes companies according to business specialty and geographical location.

500—The Directory of U.S. Corporations (Trenton, New Jersey)

Reference of Corporate Management
National directory of management personnel.

Regional Business Directory
Businesses listed by location in regional areas of the United States.

Walker's Manual of Western Corporations
Lists all corporations in the western United States alphabetically, by region. Corporate officers also listed.

Ward's Business Directory of U.S. Public and Private Companies
Alphabetical and geographical listings.

In large cities, legal newspapers usually publish a list of "100 Largest Law Firms" annually. This could be an excellent source of information on various types of law practice.

Probate Directories

The Probate Counsel (Probate Counsel, Inc., Phoenix)

Sullivan's Probate Directory (Galesburg, Illinois)

Real Estate

Land Trust Directory
Real estate magazine published by Law Bulletin Publishing Company.

Other general business directories may have specialized sections on real estate.

Legal Aid Organizations and Directories

Your city library will provide additional information regarding nonprofit organizations in your area.

National Directory of Non-Profit Companies

Public Interest Law Groups by Karen O'Connor and Lee Epstein.

Major public interest legal groups and institutional profiles are included.

Other Directories or Publications

Encyclopedia of Associations (Gale Research Co., Detroit)

National Trade and Professional Associations (Columbia Books, Inc., Washington, D.C.)

Literary Market Place (R.R. Bowker Co., New York and London)

The Writer's Market (Writer's Digest Books, Cincinnati)

The last two books on this list provide useful information for those interested in writing for publication on topics of interest to paralegals.

Legal Publications

American Bar Association Journal

Monthly news feature publication for lawyers. Special sections highlight current changes in the law. Classified ads for attorneys listed.

The American Lawyer

Profiles of current legal departments, major firms, client acquisitions, and significant cases. An in-depth survey of one hundred major firms is also published annually.

Legal Assistant Today

Legal Times: Law and Lobbying in the Nation's Capital

A weekly newspaper with national circulation. Valuable for those interested in working with the federal government.

The National Law Journal

Weekly newspaper that covers all aspects of law in the United States. Includes classified ads.

National Paralegal Reporter (Published quarterly by the National Federation of Paralegals, Inc.)

Includes articles on current issues, membership activities, seminar announcements, and classified ads.

Trial

Monthly journal for members of the Association of Trial Lawyers. Worth examining if you would like to consider working in this area.

Bar Associations and Local Publications

Each region will have offices for the following associations. Check with your local paralegal association or in your local telephone book for current addresses and telephone numbers. A space is given below for you to include this information which could be a valuable part of your job search.

Local Address and Phone Number

City Bar Association   _____

_____

American Bar Association   _____

_____

State Bar Association   _____

Local Law Journals and Newspapers   _____

_____

_____

_____

Working for the Federal Government

Federal Job Information

If you are interested in finding a paralegal position with the federal government, it is important to know how to apply and where to find information.

To find out about job openings and job qualifications, refer to the Qualifications Information Statement available in any Federal Job Information

Center listed below or at an Office of Personnel Management. The Office of Personnel Management provides federal employment information to state job service offices and to college placement offices. Many federal agencies also recruit directly for their own vacancies and provide a wide range of information services. As the central federal personnel office, the Office of Personnel Management also conducts testing for selected positions and delegates other testing responsibilities to certain agencies. Check with an Office of Personnel Management near you to find out if you can apply for open positions directly related to the specific agency. Test application forms are available at the Federal Job Information Center; you may call and request that a form be sent to you. After you submit your request to take a test, you will receive a copy of your form, including the time and location of the examination. In addition, you will receive a basic application form and a practice test.

After passing the examination, your name is placed on a competitive inventory and circulated to agencies as vacancies occur. But you may also apply directly to agencies if you meet the specific requirements listed in the Qualifications Information Statement. Additional information about your background and qualifications will also be required. You will usually have to complete another form (SF 171, a Personal Qualifications Statement), which is a standard application form for federal employment.

The Office of Personnel Management also requires you to complete their own OPM Form 1170/1171, in which you list the college courses you have taken. A transcript of your college course work may also be required.

Although it may appear that a position with the federal government is simply a series of bureaucratic activities, once you understand the process and ask the right questions, you may find just the position you are looking for.

A list of various federal government offices that hire paralegals is included in this section. These offices are not necessarily in Washington, D.C. Most departments have offices in major cities throughout the country.

If you decide to pursue this route to your paralegal career, you must be aware of how government works and fulfill all the requirements.

Be certain to complete all the necessary paper work, and be very precise in the information you include. If you have any questions, contact the appropriate agency personnel. Also pay attention to deadlines. If you miss a deadline or neglect to include all the required information, your application may be delayed or you may miss out on the position you want.

You will be informed of your eligibility (based on successfully passing the examination and having the proper qualifications). You will also be notified of vacancies when they occur. If you apply for an opening, contact the agency within two weeks to find out if your application has been received. If you apply to a Special Examining Unit, allow from four to six weeks for application processing. During that time, you will be sent a "Notice of Rating," or if sending an application directly to a hiring agency, you will be contacted for an interview if you are considered to be highly qualified.

If you are called in for an interview, review the annual report published by each agency. A copy of this report and the mission statement will be sent to you upon request. It will help you prepare for the interview. Also review the chapter on interviewing in this text for guidelines on successful interviewing.

The Office of Personnel Management publishes a list of materials that you may also request.

Handbook of Occupational Groups and Series
The section entitled "Definitions of Groups and Series Relative to Paralegal Specialists" is very useful.

Handbook X118, U.S. Government's Paralegal Hiring Standard

List of government agencies with legal departments.

Schedule of pay rates from grades GS-5 through GS-12 (GS indicates General Schedule).

Review the list of publications relating to federal government positions listed earlier in this Appendix for additional information.

Federal agencies, commissions, and departments that hire paralegals:

> Administrative Office of the United States Courts
> Agency for International Development (AID)
> Army, Department of (Defense Department)
> Bureau of Land Management (BLM) (Interior Department)
> Commission on Civil Rights
> Commodity Futures Trading Commission
> Corps of Engineer
> Defense, Department of (DOD)
> Drug Enforcement Administration (DEA) (Justice Department)
> Energy, Department of
> Equal Employment Opportunity Commission (EEOC)
> Executive Office of the President
> Federal Aviation Administration (FAA) (Transportation Department)
> Federal Communications Commission (FCC)
> Federal Deposit Insurance Corporation (FDIC)
> Federal Emergency Management Agency (FEMA)

Federal Maritime Commission
Federal Railroad Administration (Transportation Department)
Federal Reserve System, Board of Governors
Federal Retirement Thrift Investment Board
Federal Trade Commission (FTC) (Commerce Department)
General Services Administration (GSA)
Interior, Department of
International Trade Commission
Labor, Department of
Library of Congress
Merit Systems Protection Board
National Highway Traffic Safety Administration (Transportation Department)
National Labor Relations Board (NLRB)
Navy, Department of (Defense Department)
Office of Attorney Personnel Management (Justice Department)
Offices of the Secretary (Commerce Department, Health and Human Services Department)
Office of the Solicitor (Labor Department)
Office of the Solicitor General (Justice Department)
Office of Thrift Supervision (Treasury Department)
Patent and Trademark Office (Commerce Department)
Postal Service
Resolution Trust Corporation (RTC)
Securities and Exchange Commission (SEC)
Small Business Administration (SBA)
State, Department of
Transportation, Department of
Veteran Affairs, Department of

Government specialties, included in Chapter 2 of this book under Paralegal Specialties, cover a wide range of areas, depending upon the functions of the specific office.

Federal Job Information Centers

Alabama

Southerland Building
806 Governors Drive, N.W.
Huntsville, AL 35801
(205) 453-5070

Alaska

Federal Building United States Courthouse
701 C Street
PO Box 22
Anchorage, AK 99513
(907) 271-5821

Arizona

522 North Central Avenue
Phoenix, AZ 85004
(602) 261-4736

Arkansas

Federal Building, Room 1319
700 West Capitol Avenue
Little Rock, AR 72201
(501) 378-5842

California

Linder Building
650 Capitol Mall
Sacramento, CA 95814
(916) 440-3441

880 Front Street
San Diego, CA 92188
(714) 293-6165

Federal Building
845 South Figueroa
Los Angeles, CA 90017
(213) 688-3360

Federal Building Room 1001
450 Golden Avenue
San Francisco, CA 94102
(415) 556-6667

Colorado

1845 Sherman Street
Denver, CO 80203
(303) 837-3506

Connecticut

Federal Building, Room 717
450 Main Street
Hartford, CT 06103
(203) 244-3096

Delaware

Federal Building
844 King Street
Wilmington, DE 19801
(302) 571-6288

District of Columbia

1900 E. Street, N.W.
Metro Area
Washington, D.C. 20415
(202) 737-9616

Florida

330 Biscayne Blvd., Suite 340
Miami, FL 33131
(305) 350-4725

80 N. Hughey Ave.
Orlando, FL 32801
(305) 420-6148

Georgia

Richard B. Russell Federal Building
75 Spring St. S.W.
Atlanta, GA 30303
(404) 221-4315

Guam

238 O'Hara St.
Room 308
Agana, Guam 96910

Hawaii

Federal Building, Room 1310
300 Ala Moana Blvd.
Honolulu, HI 96850
(808) 546-7108

Illinois

Dirksen Building, Room 1322
219 South Dearborn Street
Chicago, IL 60604
(312) 353-5136

Indiana

46 East Ohio Street, Room 123
Indianapolis, IN 46204
(317) 269-7161 or 7162

Iowa

210 Walnut Street, Room 191
Des Moines, IA 50309
(515) 284-4546

Kansas

One-Twenty Building, Room 101
120 South Market Street
Witchita, KS 67202
(316) 267-6311, ext. 106

Kentucky

Federal Building
600 Federal Place
Louisville, KY 40202
(502) 528-5130

Louisiana

F. Edward Hebert Building
610 South Street, Room 103
New Orleans, LA 70130
(504) 589-2764

Maine

Federal Building, Room 611
Sewall Street and Western Avenue
Augusta, MA 04330
(207) 622-6171, ext.269

Maryland

Garmatz Federal Building
101 W. Lombard Street
Baltimore, MD 21201
(202) 962-3822

1900 E. Street, N.W.
DC Metro Area, MD 20415
(202) 737-9616

Massachusetts

3 Center Plaza
Boston, MA 02108
(617) 223-2571

Michigan

477 Michigan Avenue, Room 595
Detroit, MI 48226
(313) 226-6950

Minnesota

Federal Building
Ft. Snelling, St. Paul
St. Paul, MN 55111
(612) 725-3355

Mississippi

100 W. Capitol Street, Suite 335
Jackson, MS 39201
(601) 490-4588

Missouri

Federal Building and Room 129
601 East 12th Street
Kansas City, MO 64106
(816) 374-5702

Federal Building, Room 1712
1520 Market Street
St. Louis, MO 63101
(314) 425-4285

Montana

Federal Building and Courthouse
301 S. Park, Room 153
Helena, MT 59601
(406) 449-5388

Nebraska

U.S. Courthouse and Post Office Building
Room 1014
215 N. 17th St.
Omaha, NE 67102
(402) 221-3815

Nevada

Mill and S. Virginia Streets
PO Box 3296
Reno, NV 89505
(702) 784-5535

New Hampshire

Federal Building, Room 104
Daniel and Penhallow Streets
Portsmouth, NH 03801
(603) 436-7720, ext. 762

New Jersey

Federal Building
970 Broad Street
Newark, NJ 07102
(201) 645-3673
In Camden, dial (215) 597-7440

New Mexico

Federal Building
421 Gold Avenue, S.W.
Albuquerque, NM 87102
(505) 766-2557

New York

590 Grand Concourse
Bronx, NY 10451
(212) 292-4666

111 W. Huron St.
Buffalo, NY 14202
(716) 846-4001

90-04 161st Street, Room 200
Jamaica, NY 11432
(212) 264-0422

Federal Building
26 Federal Plaza
New York, NY 10278
(212)264-0422

100 South Clinton Street
Syracuse, NY 13260
(315) 423-5660

North Carolina

Federal Building
310 New Bern Avenue
PO Box 25069
Raleigh, NC 27611
(919) 755-4361

North Dakota

Federal Building, Room 202
657 Second Avenue N.
Fargo, ND 58102
(701) 237-5771, ext. 363

Ohio

Federal Building
1240 E. 9th Street
Cleveland, OH 44199
(216) 522-4232

Federal Building, Lobby
200 W. 2nd Street
Dayton, OH 45402
(513) 225-2720, 225-2854

Oklahoma

800-688-9889

Oregon

Federal Building, Lobby (North)
1220 S.W. Third Street
Portland, OR 97204
(503) 221-3141

Pennsylvania

Federal Building, Room 168
Harrisburg, PA 17108
(717) 782-4494

William J.Green, Jr.
Federal Building
600 Arch Street
Philadelphia, PA 19106
(215) 597-7440

Federal Building
1000 Liberty Avenue
Pittsburgh, PA 15222
(412) 644-2755

Puerto Rico

Federico Degetau Federal Building
Carlos E. Chardon Street
Hato Rey, P.R. 00918
(809) 753-4209 ext. 209

Rhode Island

Federal & Post Office Building Room 310
Kennedy Plaza
Providence, RI 02903

South Carolina

1550 Gadsden Street
Columbia, SC 29202
(803) 737-2400

Tennessee

Federal Building
167 North Main Street
Memphis, TN 38103
(901) 521-3956

Texas

1100 Commerce Street, Room 1C42
Dallas, TX 75242
(214) 767-8035

701 San Jacinto Street
Houston, TX 77002
(713) 226-5501

Property Trust Building, Suite N302
2211 E. Missouri Ave.
El Paso, TX 79903
(915) 543-7425

643 E. Durango Blvd.
San Antonio, TX 78205
(512) 229-6600

Utah

1234 South Main Street, 2nd Floor
Salt Lake City, UT 84101
(801) 524-5744

Vermont

Federal Building, Room 614
PO Box 489
Elmwood Ave. and Pearl Street
Burlington, VT 05402
(801) 524-5744

Virginia

Federal Building, Room 220
200 Granby Mall
Norfolk, VA 23510
(804) 441-3355

1900 E. Street, N.W.
D.C. Metro Area, VA 20415
(202) 737-9616

Washington

Federal Building
915 Second Avenue
Seattle, WA 98174
(206) 442-4365

West Virginia

Federal Building
500 Quarrier Street
Charleston, WV 253301
(304) 343-6181, ext. 226

Wisconsin

Plankinton Building, Room 205
161 West Wisconsin Avenue
Milwaukee, WI 53203
(414) 244-3761

Wyoming

2120 Capitol Ave., Room 304
PO Box 967
Cheyenne, WY 82001
(307) 778-2220 ext. 2108

Paralegal Associations

Paralegal associations can be a valuable resource for all paralegals. They are a great source of networking contacts. Many state or local associations have job bank committees that list current job opportunities. Most offer programs to help the paralegal just starting out or provide insights and information to both new and experienced paralegals. These professional associations frequently provide a forum for discussing important topics, including ethics, standards, current issues in the profession and continuing legal education.

Take advantage of all that your local paralegal association can offer. This list includes major locations of paralegal associations, but additional ones may exist in various states. For further information, or for the address of an association closer to you, contact the ones listed here or ask someone in a paralegal training program to help you locate one. Be certain to check for any changes in address.

National Associations

American Academy of Legal Assistants
Professional Arts Building
1022 Park Avenue, N.E.
Norton, VA 24273

American Association for Paralegal Education
PO Box 40244
Overland Park, KS 66204

American Paralegal Association
PO Box 35233
Los Angeles, CA 74105

Legal Assistant Management Association
PO Box 40129
Overland Park, KS 66204

National Association of Legal Assistants, Inc.
PO Box 7587
Tulsa, OK 74105

National Federation of Paralegal Associations
104 Wilmot Road, Suite 201
Deerfield, IL 60015-5195

National Indian Paralegal Association
7524 Major Avenue North
Brooklyn Park, MN 55443

National Paralegal Association
60 East State Street
Doylestown, PA 18901

Alabama

Alabama Association of Legal Assistants
PO Box 55727
Birmingham, AL 35255

Legal Assistant Society of Southern Institute
2015 Highland Avenue South
Birmingham, AL 35205

Mobile Association of Legal Assistants
PO Box 1852
Mobile, AL 36623

Alabama Association of Legal Assistants
PO Box 2069
Montgomery, AL 36197

Alaska

Alaska Legal Assistants Association
PO Box 1956
Anchorage, AK 99510

Fairbanks Association of Legal Assistants
PO Box 73503
Fairbanks, AK 99707

Arizona

Tucson Association of Legal Assistants
PO Box 257
Tucson, AZ 85702

Arizona Paralegal Association
PO Box 13083
Phoenix, AZ 85002

Northern Arizona Paralegal Association
Northern Arizona University
PO Box 7692
Flagstaff, AZ 86001

Arizona Paralegal Association
1201 S. Alma School Road
Suite 15500
Mesa, AZ 85210

Arkansas

Arkansas Association of Legal Assistants
2200 Worthen Bank Building
Little Rock, AR 72201

California

California Alliance of Paralegal Associations
PO Box 26383
San Francisco, CA 94126

California Public Sector Paralegal Association
Stockton Street, Suite 400
San Francisco, CA 94133

Central Coast Legal Assistants Association
PO Box 1582
San Luis Obispo, CA 93406

Channel Cities Legal Assistants Association
PO Box 1260
Santa Barbara, CA 93120

Orange County Paralegal Association
PO Box 8512
Newport Beach, CA 92658

Paralegal Association of San Mateo County
250 Wheeler Avenue
Redwood City, CA 94061

Paralegal Association of Santa Clara County
PO Box 26736
San Jose, CA 95159

Sacramento Association of Legal Assistants
PO Box 453
Sacramento, CA 95802

East Bay Association of Legal Assistants
PO Box 424
Oakland, CA 94604

Los Angeles Paralegal Association
PO Box 24350
Los Angeles, CA 90024

San Diego Association of Legal Assistants
PO Box 12508
San Diego, CA 92112

San Francisco Association of Legal Assistants
PO Box 26668
San Francisco, CA 94126

Colorado

Legal Assistants of Colorado
PO Box 628
Gunnison, CO 81230

Rocky Mountain Legal Assistants Association
PO Box 304
Denver, CO 81230

Connecticut

Connecticut Association of Paralegals, Fairfield County
PO Box 134
Bridgeport, CT 06601

Central Connecticut Association of Legal Assistants
PO Box 230594
Hartford, CT 06123-0594

Connecticut Association of Paralegals, New Haven
PO Box 862
New Haven, CT 06504-0862

Delaware

Delaware Paralegal Association
PO Box 1362
Wilmington, DE 19899

District of Columbia

National Capital Area Paralegal Association
1155 Connecticut Ave., N.W.
Washington, D.C. 20036

Florida

Broward County Paralegal Association
Ruden, Barnett, McCloskey, et al.
PO Box 1900
Ft. Lauderdale, FL 33302

Jacksonville Legal Assistants
PO Box 52264
Jacksonville, FL 32201

Florida Legal Assistants, Inc.
Director, Region VII
4221 Cherry Laurel Drive
Pensacola, FL 32504

Dade Association of Legal Assistants
700 Brickell Avenue
Miami, FL 33133

Georgia

Georgia Association of Legal Assistants
PO Box 1802
Atlanta, GA 30301

Hawaii

Hawaii Association of Legal Assistants
PO Box 674
Honolulu, HI 96809

Idaho

Boise Association of Lawyer's Assistants
PO Box 50
Boise, ID 83728

Intermountain Paralegal Association
PO Box 6009
Pocatello, ID 83205-6009

Illinois

Illinois Paralegal Association
PO Box 857
Chicago, IL 60690

Indiana

Indiana Legal Assistants
230 East Ohio Street
Sixth Floor
Indianapolis, IN 46204

Indianapolis Paralegal Association
PO Box 44518
Federal Station
Indianapolis, IN 46204

Iowa

Iowa Legal Assistants Association
PO Box 335
Des Moines, IA 50302

Paralegals of Iowa, Ltd.
3324 Kimball Ave.
Waterloo, IA 50702

Kansas

Kansas Association of Legal Assistants
700 Fourth Financial Center
Wichita, KS 67202

Kansas Legal Assistants Society
1174 S.W. Fillmore
Topeka, KS 66604

Kentucky

Kentucky Paralegal Association
PO Box 34503
Louisville, KY 40232

Louisville Association of Paralegals
PO Box 962
Louisville, KY 40201

Louisiana

New Orleans Paralegal Association
PO Box 30604
New Orleans, LA 70190

Baton Rouge Paralegal Association
PO Box 306
Baton Rouge, LA 70821

Maine

Maine Association of Paralegals
DTS PO Box 7554
Portland, ME 04111

Maine Paralegal Association
Union Mutual Life Insurance
2211 Congress Street
Portland, ME 04112

Maryland

Baltimore Association of Legal Assistants
PO Box 1653
Baltimore, MD 21203

Massachusetts

Massachusetts Paralegal Association
PO Box 423
Boston, MA 02102

Berkshire Association for Paralegals and Legal Secretaries
Grinnell and Dubendorf
PO Box 576
Williamstown, MA 02167

Central Massachusetts Paralegal Association
PO Box 444
Worcester, MA 01614

Michigan

Legal Assistant Association of Michigan
PO Box 12306
Birmingham, MI 48012

Michigan Association of Legal Assistants
17371 Collinson St.
East Detroit, MI 48201

Minnesota

Arrowhead Association of Legal Assistants
PO Box 221
Duluth, MN 55801

Minnesota Association of Legal Assistants
PO Box 15165
Minneapolis, MN 55415

Mississippi

Mississippi Association of Legal Assistants
PO Box 966
Jackson, MS 39205

Missouri

Kansas City Association of Legal Assistants
PO Box 13223
Kansas City, MO 64199

St. Louis Association of Legal Assistants
PO Box 8705
St. Louis, MO 63102

Nebraska

Nebraska Association of Legal Assistants
PO Box 81434
Lincoln, NE 68501

New Jersey

New Jersey Legal Assistants Association
Central Jersey Paralegal Division
PO Box 403, U.S. Hwy 30
Dayton, NJ 08810

Paralegal Association of Central Jersey
93 Princeton Court
Mercerville, NJ 08021

New Jersey Paralegal Association
232 Inza Street
Highland PK, NJ 08904

South Jersey Paralegal Association
412 East Linden Ave.
Lindenwold, NJ 08021

New Mexico

Legal Assistants of New Mexico
PO Box 1945
Albuquerque, NM 87103

New York

Central New York Paralegal Association
Bond, Schoeneck and King
One Lincoln Center
Syracuse, NY 13204

New York City Paralegal Association
FDR Station, PO Box 5143
New York, NY 10022

Paralegal Association of Rochester
700 Midtown Tower
Rochester, NY 14604

North Carolina

Cumberland County Paralegal Association
PO Box 1358
Fayetteville, NC 28302

Metrolina Paralegal Association
PO Box 32397
Charlotte, NC 28232

North Carolina Paralegal Association
PO Box 10214
Raleigh, NC 27605

Paralegal Association of Charlotte
1130 East Third Street
Charlotte, NC 28280

Raleigh-Wake Forest Paralegal Association
PO Box 10096
Raleigh, NC 27605

North Dakota

Red River Valley Legal Assistants
PO Box 1954
Fargo, ND 58102

Western Dakota Association of Legal Assistants
PO Box 1366
Williston, ND 58801

Ohio

Cincinnati Paralegal Association
PO Box 1515
Cincinnati, OH 45201

Cleveland Association of Paralegals
PO Box 14247
Cleveland, OH 44144

Legal Assistants of Central Ohio
PO Box 15182
Columbus, OH 43216

Toledo Association of Legal Assistants
PO Box 1842, Central Station
Toledo, OH 43612

Greater Dayton Paralegal Association
PO Box 515
Mid City Station
Dayton, OH 45402

Oklahoma

Oklahoma Paralegal Association
PO Box 1108
Enid, OK 73702

Tulsa Association of Legal Assistants
4100 BOK Tower
Tulsa, OK 74172

Oregon

Oregon Legal Assistants Association
PO Box 8523
Portland, OR 97207

Willamette Valley Paralegals, Inc.
Bohemia, Inc.
2280 Oakmont Way
Eugene, OR 97401

Pennsylvania

Paralegal Association of N.W. Pennsylvania
PO Box 1504
Erie, PA 16507

Central Pennsylvania Paralegal Association
PO Box 11814
Harrisburg, PA 17108

Philadelphia Association of Paralegals
1411 Walnut Street, Suite 200
Philadelphia, PA 19102

Pittsburgh Paralegal Association
PO Box 1053
Pittsburgh, PA 15203

Puerto Rico

Puerto Rico Association of Legal Assistants
GPO Box 4225
San Juan, PR 00936

Rhode Island

Rhode Island Paralegal Association
PO Box 1003
Providence, RI 02901

South Carolina

Carolina Paralegal Association
7437 Highview Rd.
Columbia, SC 29204

South Dakota

South Dakota Legal Assistants Association, Inc.
PO Box 2670
Rapid City, SD 57709

Tennessee

East Tennessee Association of Legal Assistants
3370 Jackson Circle, S.E.
Cleveland, TN 37311

Memphis Paralegal Association
PO Box 3646
Memphis, TN 38103

Tennessee Valley Legal Assistants Association
507 Gay Street, S.W.
Knoxville, TN 37902

East Tennessee Paralegal Association
450 Maclellan Building
Chattanooga, TN 37402

Texas

Alamo Area Professional Legal Assistants, Inc.
PO Box 524
San Antonio, TX 78292

Capital Area Paralegal Association
111 Congress, Suite 1700
Austin, TX 78701

Fort Worth Paralegal Association
PO Box 17021
Fort Worth, TX 77052

Houston Legal Assistants Association
PO Box 52241
Houston, TX 77052

Dallas Association of Legal Assistants
PO Box 117885
Carrollton, TX 75011-7885

Texas Panhandle Association of Legal Assistants
PO Box 15525
Amarillo, TX 79105

Nueces County Association of Legal Assistants
800 Bayview Federal Building
Corpus Christi, TX 78474

West Texas Association of Legal Assistants
PO Box 1499
Lubbock, TX 79408

Texarkana Association of Legal Assistants
PO Box 5367
Texarkana, TX 75505-5367

Utah

Legal Assistants of Utah
PO Box 112001
Salt Lake City, UT 84125

Virginia

Shenandoah Valley Paralegal Association
PO Box 88
Harrisonburg, VA 22801

Richmond Association of Legal Assistants
McGuire, Woods and Battle
One James Center
Richmond, VA 23219

Roanoke Valley Paralegal Association
PO Box 1018
Roanoke, VA 24005

Paralegal Association of Virginia
PO Box 1081
Emporia, VA 23847

Central Virginia Legal Assistants Association
PO Box 4461
Lynchburg, VA 24502

Virgin Islands

Virgin Islands Paralegals
PO Box 9121
St. Thomas, VI 00801

Washington

Washington Legal Assistants Association
2033 6th Avenue
Suite 804
Seattle, WA 98121

West Virginia

Legal Assistants of West Virginia, Inc.
Jackson and Kelly
PO Box 553
Charleston, WV 25322-0553

Wisconsin

Paralegal Association of Wisconsin
PO Box 92882
Milwaukee, WI 53202

Wyoming

Legal Assistants of Wyoming
c/o Brown and Drew
Casper Business Center
Suite 800
123 West First Street
Casper, WY 82601

Wyoming Legal Assistant Association
HC 31, Box 2746H
Riverton, WY 82501

Additional Sources of Job Leads

Local and National Newspapers, Legal and Nonlegal
- Classified advertisements
- News stories
- Position wanted ads

Professional Organizations

Job Fairs and Newsletters
- American Bar Association
- State and County Bar Associations
- Regional Paralegal Associations

College and Law School Placement Offices

Trade Associations

Political Organizations

Religious Organizations

Women's Organizations

Court House Bulletins

Chambers of Commerce

Libraries

Professional Journals, Legal and Nonlegal

Yellow Pages of Telephone Directories

Recommended Reading

Bolles, Richard. *What Color is Your Parachute?* Berkeley: Ten Speed Press, 1995.

Berkey, Rachel Lane, "Finding Employment," *Legal Assistant Today* (Spring, 1995).

Covey, Stephen. *The 7 Habits of Highly Effective People.* New York: Simon & Schuster, 1989.

Howard, Terry. "Challenging Government Jobs for the Paralegal," *Legal Assistant Today* (May/June, 1991).

Krantz, Les. *The Jobs-Rated Almanac.* Mahwahn: World Almanac, 1990.

Morrison, Laura, and Gina DeCiani. *Legal Ethics for Paralegals and the Law Office.* St. Paul: West Publishing Company, 1995.

Raye-Johnson, Vanda. *Effective Networking.* Palo Alto: Crisp Publications, 1990.

Statsky, William. *Paralegal Ethics and Regulations.* 2d Edition. St.Paul: West Publishing, 1993.

Wright, John W. and Edward S. Dwyer. *American Almanac of Jobs and Salaries.* New York: Avon Books, 1990.

Appendix B: Job Search Notebook, Checklists, and Logs

Job Search Notebook

This notebook offers a series of reminders to help you in the final stages of your job search. The checklists for each section serve to check the completion and accuracy of specific information. Final recommendations will add to the professionalism of your material.

Resume Checklist

❏ *Appearance*
   ❏ Color _____
   ❏ Weight _____

❏ *Format*
   ❏ Production Choice
      ❏ Typeset _____
      ❏ Laser Printing _____

❏ *Quantity* _____

❏ *Cost (per 100)* _____

❏ *Due Dates* _____
   ❏ Assignment date (if relevant) _____
   ❏ Printer delivery date _____

❏ *Content*
   (Check when completed.)
   ❏ Accuracy (verification of names, dates) _____
   ❏ Editing (spelling, grammar, usage, style) _____
   ❏ Proofreading _____

Resume

Portfolio of Writing Samples

The following guidelines will help you as you develop a portfolio of writing samples.

1. Select the most appropriate examples of professional writing *you* have done at your job or as part of your course work at school.

2. Clearly identify the type or purpose of the writing sample (such as its intended audience or reason it was assigned).

3. Type all samples (laser printout is acceptable.) Handwritten writing samples should be typed for your portfolio.

4. Proofread each sample carefully to avoid spelling, grammatical, or typing errors.

5. Choose works that are brief, focused, and achieve the purpose for which they were written. It is better to have shorter samples that are one or two pages long and include more of them.

6. Avoid *personal* topics or controversial issues in selecting content areas.

7. Have a former professor or respected colleague evaluate materials before including them in your portfolio.

8. Do not violate confidentiality. If real names and events are referred to, delete the specifics or change the details or request permission to use such information.

9. Make certain all materials have a professional appearance. Submit only clean copies of class papers, reports, memos (or any other materials that have been circulated).

The following types of writing could serve as samples in your portfolio:

- A legal research memo or report
- A motion
- A set of interrogatories
- Answers to a set of interrogatories
- An index to discovery documents
- An appellate brief
- An intake memorandum of law
- An answer to a problem in the textbook
- A digest of one or more discovery documents
- Sample reports or studies

Ask teachers and supervisors to select samples that best represent your writing style. You may include remarks, comments, and grades, if they provide a positive evaluation of your work.

References

The final line of your resumé indicates that references are available upon request. The following guidelines may help you to choose the most appropriate references. Contact these references as soon as you begin your job search to obtain permission to use their names. Finally, be certain to inform your references when you accept a position, and thank them in a letter for their help in your job search.

Types of References

1. Usually, three or four references are requested on a job application.
2. The best references will be people who know you and can genuinely support you for a position.
3. Professional references may include: teachers, former employers, project directors, or professional colleagues.
4. Professional references should be able to do the following:

   - Address your strengths, weaknesses, and potential for growth.

   - Vouch for your job performance and work habits.

   - Comment on your personal and professional characteristics and qualifications, such as reliability, initiative, commitment. and integrity.

5. Personal references (if requested) should address your honesty, integrity, reputation in the community, and so forth.
6. If you have limited job experience, rely on a reference who has seen your work either on a special project (part-time or volunteer) in or out of class.
7. Choose your references as they relate to the position for which you are applying.

   - Choose someone who knows you and your work in the legal field.

   - Choose someone who has observed you in a position that required the same or similar qualifications required of a paralegal (working with details, deadlines, clients, and so forth.)

8. Aim for a variety of references if you have limited work experience, so that the employer has verification of your abilities as well as capabilities.

It will be very helpful to your references if you send them a copy of your resumé. They will be able to guide their remarks accordingly, if they are

It will be very helpful to your references if you send them a copy of your resumé. They will be able to guide their remarks accordingly, if they are aware of your background and accomplishments.

Reminders

1. Employers *will* check your references. So be certain to contact references for permission and inform them about the job or jobs for which you will be applying, so they can think about why you would be a good candidate.

2. If you are writing to someone to ask for permission to use him or her as a reference, identify how and in what context you know the person. For example, mention the class you attended, specific papers or projects you worked on, or any other details that could help the person recall your specific qualifications.

3. In requesting permission from a former boss or supervisor, refresh that person's memory (particularly if the job was not in the recent past) by recalling the specific dates of your employment and in what capacity you worked. Sending them a current resumé will also be helpful.

4. If you are unable to contact a former employer or if you have reason to believe that you would not receive a favorable recommendation and if that job was a significant part of your work history, ask a former colleague who knows your work well to serve as a reference for that particular employment period.

First-hand observation of a job applicant is very useful to an employer. And if you remember that employers are looking for a person with the *personal,* as well as *professional,* qualifications, you will choose references who can comment on both aspects. Remember that employers are looking for someone who will fit into the organization and be able to get along with the other employees.

References can and should be a valuable asset to your job search. Do not take them for granted. Always extend professional courtesy by contacting them for permission before you apply for the job and after you accept a position to let them know the results of your search.

Job Sources Checklist

❏ Friends and relatives in paralegal or legal profession _____
❏ Teachers _____
❏ Colleagues or former colleagues _____
❏ Alumni associations _____
❏ Community or civic associations _____
❏ Job fairs _____

❐ Job directories _____
❐ Legal secretaries _____
❐ Legal administrators _____
❐ General directories of attorneys _____
❐ Special directories of attorneys _____
❐ Placement offices _____
  ❐ Colleges and universities _____
  ❐ Local law schools _____
❐ Government job listings _____
❐ Newspapers and newsletters _____
  ❐ Want ads or circulation of daily papers _____
  ❐ Legal newspapers _____
  ❐ Paralegal newsletters _____
❐ Bulletins of all civic or community professional organizations _____
❐ Professional associations _____
  ❐ Paralegal associations _____
  ❐ Business and management associations _____
  ❐ Specialty fields associations _____
  ❐ Employment agencies _____

Job Search Calendar

Letters Checklist		
Type of Letter	**Date Sent and Where Sent**	**Date of Response Received/**
Reference request (may be a telephone request)		
Cover letter		
Follow-up letter ■ Job contact thank you ■ Informational interview ■ Job interview		
Job acceptance letter		

Job Contact Log

Contact	Position	Action Taken	Date

Interview Log and Self-Evaluation Chart

Interview Date	Name of Firm	Positive Points	Negative Points

Job Listings and Action Taken

(Written or Telephone correspondence)

Date	Place	Action Taken

Interview Checklist (For personal or job information preparation)

- ❏ Specific job or position _____
- ❏ Organization or firm _____
- ❏ Location _____ Time of interview _____
- ❏ Name of interviewer _____
- ❏ Transportation:
  - ❏ Public (time schedule) _____
  - ❏ Auto (parking facilities) _____
  - ❏ Confirmed directions _____
- ❏ Departure time _____
- ❏ Arrival time _____
- ❏ Dress code _____
- ❏ Resume copies _____
- ❏ Writing samples portfolio _____
- ❏ Reference list _____

Information on Position

- ❏ Employer specialty _____
- ❏ Duties and responsibilities of paralegal position _____
  _____
- ❏ Required training, experience, education _____
- ❏ Supervisory structure _____
- ❏ Methods of supervision _____
- ❏ Support staff (clerical, etc.)
- ❏ Client contact _____
- ❏ Career opportunities _____
- ❏ Performance evaluation _____
- ❏ Continuing education: Required _____   Support _____
  Reimbursement _____
- ❏ Billable hours expected of paralegals _____
- ❏ Travel _____
- ❏ Overtime _____
- ❏ Compensation and benefits (salary, bonus, health plan, life insurance, sick leave, vacation, maternity leave, parking, and so forth)
- ❏ Decision deadline: Employer _____ Applicant acceptance _____

Interview Self-Evaluation Checklist

(May be duplicated and used for each job interview)

Position and Organization	Date	Positive or Negative Evaluation of Interview

❏ I would/would not like this position _____

❏ I was/was not satisfied with the interview _____

❏ Difficult questions asked

_____

_____

❏ Self-evaluation of responses:

❏ Improved responses (for next interview)

❏ Follow-up letter(s) sent _____
   ❏ Letter or response received _____
   ❏ Second interview _____

❏ Interview results

❏ Job offered _____   ❏ Job not offered _____
❏ Declined _____   ❏ Reasons _____

❏ Accepted _____

   ❏ Starting date _____
   ❏ Salary_____
   ❏ Benefits _____

❏ Other comments:

Expense Sheet

Item	Amount	Date
Stationery		
Business Cards		
Contracts		
Postage		
Supplies (list)		
Travel Expenses		
Telephone		
Office equipment (list)		
Professional dues or memberships		
Other		

Income Sheet

Received From	Payment For	Date	Amount	Balance Due

Appendix C: The NALA and NFPA Codes of Ethics and Professional Responsibility

Preamble

A legal assistant must adhere strictly to the accepted standards of legal ethics and to the general principles of proper conduct. The performance of the duties of the legal assistant shall be governed by specific canons as defined herein so that justice will be served and goals of the profession attained. (See NALA Model Standards and Guidelines for Utilization of Legal Assistants, Section II.)

The canons of ethics set forth hereafter are adopted by the National Association of Legal Assistants, Inc., as a general guide intended to aid legal assistants and attorneys. The enumeration of these rules does not mean there are not others of equal importance although not specifically mentioned. Court rules, agency rules and statutes must be taken into consideration when interpreting the canons.

Definition

Legal assistants, also known as paralegals, are a distinguishable group of persons who assist attorneys in the delivery of legal services. Through formal education, training, and experience, legal assistants have knowledge

203

and expertise regarding the legal system and substantive and procedural law which qualify them to do work of a legal nature under the supervision of an attorney.

Canon I

A legal assistant must not perform any of the duties that attorneys only may perform nor take any actions that attorneys may not take.

Canon II

A legal assistant may perform any task which is properly delegated and supervised by an attorney, as long as the attorney is ultimately responsible to the client, maintains a direct relationship with the client, and assumes professional responsibility for the work product. (See NALA Model Standards and Guidelines for Utilization of Legal Assistants, Sections IV and VII.)

Canon III

A legal assistant must not (See NALA Model Standards and Guidelines for Utilization of Legal Assistants, Section VI):

a) engage in, encourage, or contribute to any act which could constitute the unauthorized practice of law;

b) establish attorney-client relationships, set fees, give legal opinions or advise or represent a client before a court or agency unless so authorized by that court or agency; and

c) engage in conduct or take any action which would assist or involve the attorney in a violation of professional ethics or give the appearance of professional impropriety.

Canon IV

A legal assistant must use discretion and professional judgment commensurate with knowledge and experience but must not render independent legal judgment in place of an attorney. The services of an attorney are essential in the public interest whenever such legal judgment is required. (See NALA Model Standards and Guidelines for Utilization of Legal Assistants, Section VII.)

Canon V

A legal assistant must disclose his or her status as a legal assistant at the outset of any professional relationship with a client, attorney, a court or administrative agency or personnel thereof, or a member of the general public. A legal assistant must act prudently in determining the extent to which a client may be assisted without the presence of an attorney. (See NALA Model Standards and Guidelines for Utilization of Legal Assistants, Section V.)

Canon VI

A legal assistant must strive to maintain integrity and a high degree of competency through education and training with respect to professional responsibility, local rules and practice, and through continuing education in substantive areas of law to better assist the legal profession in fulfilling its duty to provide legal services.

Canon VII

A legal assistant must protect the confidences of a client and must not violate any rule or statute now in effect or hereafter enacted controlling the doctrine of privileged communications between a client and an attorney. (See NALA Model Standards and Guidelines for Utilization of Legal Assistants, Section V.)

Canon VIII

A legal assistant must do all other things incidental, necessary, or expedient for the attainment of the ethics and responsibilities as defined by statute or rule of court.

Canon IX

A legal assistant's conduct is guided by bar associations' codes of professional responsibility and rules of professional conduct.

Adopted May 1, 1975
Revised 1979; 1988; 1995

The NFPA Model Code

Preamble

The National Federation of Paralegal Associations, Inc. ("NFPA") is a professional organization comprised of paralegal associations and individual paralegals throughout the United States. Members of the NFPA have varying types of backgrounds, experience, education, and job responsibilities which reflect the diversity of the paralegal profession. NFPA promotes the growth, development and recognition of the paralegal profession as an integral partner in the delivery of legal services.

NFPA recognizes that the creation of guidelines and standards for professional conduct are important for the development and expansion of the paralegal profession. In May 1993, NFPA adopted this Model Code of Ethics and Professional Responsibility ("Model Code") to delineate the principles for ethics and conduct to which every paralegal should aspire. The Model Code expresses NFPA's commitment to increasing the quality and efficiency of legal services and recognizes the profession's responsibilities to the public, the legal community, and colleagues.

Paralegals perform many different functions, and these functions differ greatly among practice areas. In addition, each jurisdiction has its own unique legal authority and practices governing ethical conduct and professional responsibility.

It is essential that each paralegal strive for personal and professional excellence and encourage the professional development of other paralegals as well as those entering the profession. Participation in professional associations intended to advance the quality and standards of the legal profession is of particular importance. Paralegals should possess integrity, professional skill and dedication to the improvement of the legal system and should strive to expand the paralegal role in the delivery of legal services.

Canon 1

A paralegal[1] shall achieve and maintain a high level of competence.

EC–1.1 A paralegal shall achieve competency through education, training, and work experience.

---

1. "Paralegal" is synonymous with **"Legal Assistant"** and is defined as a person qualified through education, training, or work experience to perform substantive legal work that requires knowledge of legal concepts and is customarily, but not exclusively performed by a lawyer. This person may be retained or employed by a lawyer, law office, governmental agency or other entity or may be authorized by administrative, statutory, or court authority to perform this work.

EC–1.2 A paralegal shall participate in continuing education to keep informed of current legal, technical and general developments.

EC–1.3 A paralegal shall perform all assignments promptly and efficiently.

Canon 2

A paralegal shall maintain a high level of personal and professional integrity.

EC–2.1 A paralegal shall not engage in any *ex parte*[2] communications involving the courts for any other adjudicatory body in an attempt to exert undue influence or to obtain advantage for the benefit of only one party.

EC–2.2 A paralegal shall not communicate, or cause another to communicate, with a party the paralegal knows to be represented by a lawyer in a pending matter without the prior consent of the lawyer representing such other party.

EC–2.3 A paralegal shall ensure that all timekeeping and billing records prepared by the paralegal are thorough, accurate, and honest.

EC–2.4 A paralegal shall be scrupulous, thorough and honest in the identification and maintenance of all funds, securities, and other assets of a client and shall provide accurate accountings as appropriate.

EC–2.5 A paralegal shall advise the proper authority of any dishonest or fraudulent acts by any person pertaining to the handling of the funds, securities or other assets of a client.

Canon 3

A paralegal shall maintain a high standard of professional conduct.

EC–3.1 A paralegal shall refrain from engaging in any conduct that offends the dignity and decorum of proceedings before a court or other adjudicatory body and shall be respectful of all rules and procedures.

EC–3.2 A paralegal shall advise the proper authority of any action of another legal professional which clearly demonstrates fraud, deceit, dishonesty, or misrepresentation.

EC–3.3 A paralegal shall avoid impropriety and the appearance of impropriety.

---

2. ***Ex Parte*** denotes actions or communications conducted at the instance and for the benefit of one party only, and without notice to, or contestation by, any person adversely interested.

Canon 4

A paralegal shall serve the public interest by contributing to the delivery of quality legal services and the improvement of the legal system.

EC–4.1 A paralegal shall be sensitive to the legal needs of the public and shall promote the development and implementation of programs that address those needs.

EC–4.2 A paralegal shall support bona fide efforts to meet the need for legal services by those unable to pay reasonable or customary fees; for example, participation in *pro bono* projects and volunteer work.

EC–4.3 A paralegal shall support efforts to improve the legal system and shall assist in making changes.

Canon 5

A paralegal shall preserve all confidential information[3] provided by the client or acquired from other sources before, during, and after the course of the professional relationship.

EC–5.1 A paralegal shall be aware of and abide by all legal authority governing confidential information.

EC–5.2 A paralegal shall not use confidential information to the disadvantage of the client.

EC–5.3 A paralegal shall not use confidential information to the advantage of the paralegal or of a third person.

EC–5.4 A paralegal may reveal confidential information only after full disclosure and with the client's written consent; or, when required by law or court order; or, when necessary to prevent the client from committing an act which could result in death or serious bodily harm.

EC–5.5 A paralegal shall keep those individuals responsible for the legal representation of a client fully informed of any confidential information the paralegal may have pertaining to that client.

EC–5.6 A paralegal shall not engage in any indiscreet communications concerning clients.

---

3. **"Confidential Information"** denotes information relating to a client, whatever its source, which is not public knowledge nor available to the public. (**"Non-Confidential Information"** would generally include the name of the client and the identity of the matter for which the paralegal provided services.)

Canon 6

A paralegal's title shall be fully disclosed.[4]

EC–6.1 A paralegal's title shall clearly indicate the individual's status and shall be disclosed in all business and professional communications to avoid misunderstandings and misconceptions about the paralegal's role and responsibilities.

EC–6.2 A paralegal's title shall be included if the paralegal's name appears on business cards, letterhead, brochures, directories, and advertisements.

Canon 7

A paralegal shall not engage in the unauthorized practice of law.

EC–7.1 A paralegal shall comply with the applicable legal authority governing the unauthorized practice of law.

Canon 8

A paralegal shall avoid conflicts of interest and shall disclose any possible conflict to the employer or client, as well as to the prospective employers or clients.

EC–8.1 A paralegal shall act within the bounds of the law, solely for the benefit of the client, and shall be free of compromising influences and loyalties. Neither the paralegal's personal or business interest, nor those of other clients or third persons, should compromise the paralegal's professional judgment and loyalty to the client.

EC–8.2 A paralegal shall avoid conflicts of interest which may arise from previous assignments whether for a present or past employer or client.

EC–8.3 A paralegal shall avoid conflicts of interest which may arise from family relationships and from personal and business interests.

EC–8.4 A paralegal shall create and maintain an effective recordkeeping system that identifies clients, matters, and parties with which the paralegal has worked, to be able to determine whether an actual or potential conflict of interest exists.

---

4. **"Disclose"** denotes communication of information reasonably sufficient to permit identification of the significance of the matter in question.

EC–8.5 A paralegal shall reveal sufficient nonconfidential information about a client or former client to reasonably ascertain if an actual or potential conflict of interest exists.

EC–8.6 A paralegal shall not participate in or conduct work on any matter where a conflict of interest has been identified.

EC–8.7 In matters where a conflict of interest has been identified and the client consents to continued representation, a paralegal shall comply fully with the implementation and maintenance of an Ethical Wall.[5]

---

5. **"Ethical Wall"** refers to the screening method implemented in order to protect a client from a conflict of interest. An Ethical Wall generally includes, but is not limited to, the following elements: (1) prohibit the paralegal from having any connection with the matter; (2) ban discussions with or the transfer of documents to or from the paralegal; (3) restrict access to files; and (4) educate all members of the firm, corporation or entity as to the separation of the paralegal (both organizationally and physically) from the pending matter. For more information regarding the Ethical Wall, see the NFPA publication entitled "The Ethical Wall—Its Application to Paralegals."

Source: The National Federation of Paralegal Associations.

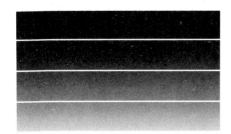

Index